Front and back:
Tutankhamun's Gold Mask (n° 256a)
The Cairo Museum.

Pages 2/3 :
Painted stucco wood casket (n° 21)
The Cairo Museum.

Page 7 :
Canopic jar top emblazoned
with the image of Tutankhamun (n° 266c to f)
The Cairo Museum.

Page 9 :
Lion-head vase (n° 579)
The Cairo Museum.

Page 120 :
Sema-tawi perfume vase (n° 210)
The Cairo Museum.

Page 129 :
Perfume vase topped by a lion-head (n° 211)
The Cairo Museum.

Page 131 :
Detail of Tutankhamun's throne (n° 91)
The Cairo Museum.

All rights reseved
© MOLIÈRE 2001, Paris
ISBN: 2.907670.36.0
Printed and bound in Italy

Photographic credits:

R. M. N.: 13, 15, 17.

J. de Beler : 2/3, 19, 21, 23, 25, 27, 45, 46, 47, 51, 54, 55, 57, 58/59, 65, 67, 69, 70, 75, 77, 93, 95, 99, 111, 120, 129, 131, 134/135.

J.-M. Biais : 94.

Giraudon : 1, 7, 8, 9, 11, 48, 53, 61, 63, 65, 78, 79, 83, 87, 88/89, 96, 97, 102, 103, 105, 106, 107, 108/109, 114/115, 117, 136.

Griffith Institute, Ashmolean Museum, Oxford : 41.

The Metropolitan Museum of Art, New York, photography by Egyptian Expedition : 34/35.

J.-C. Golvin(© Éditions Errance) : 38/39.

Times Newspapers : 30/31, 32, 33..

Text: Aude Gros de Beler.
Collaboration: F. B.S.B.

TUTANKHAMUN

Aude Gros de Beler

Foreword
Aly Maher el Sayed

MOLIÈRE

TUTANKHAMUN

Aude Gros de Beler

Foreword
Aly Maher el Sayed

FOREWORD

What a strange destiny for a fragile child to find himself, at the age of nine, hurled on to the Throne of Egypt bearing the name Tut Ankh Aten, the "living image of the God Aten". He very zealously stands up against the heresy of his predecessor, proclaims and restores the worship of the true god, Amun, the traditional supreme god... The young pharaoh then becomes Tut Ankh Amun, "living image of the God Amun"...

The god Amun regains his supremacy at the summit of the supernatural structure... The earthly and the divine worlds of beyond are once again joined together ... Effigies and idols are restored, and Amun's name, which the heretics had erased and replaced with the name of Aten on all temples, was reinstated, divine boats were reconstructed anew... Harmony and happiness were sought in Tutankhamun's name, after having been lost as the eternal gods were cast aside, ignored and offended during the heretic pharaoh Akhenaten's reign, and had become bitter and turned against impious men and the country as a whole. Now Amun's priests found their prestige, their fortune and their power restored.

The glory of this young child-King, this Pharaoh-God, derives from his return to the natural divine order, placing the supreme being back where he should always have been. His premature death shortened his reign to only nine years, nonetheless this did not prevent him from entering history as a Great Pharaoh.

Yet it was beyond his life, after his death that Tutankhamun came into his greatest glory, and ensured that his name would be remembered eternally... On the 27th of November 1922 his royal hypogeum was opened in the heart of the Valley of the Kings, to the total amazement of all Egyptologists... This sacred tomb was the only royal tomb that had been preserved and spared, with its sacrosanct sculptures, containing a mass of sacred objects, fabulous treasures, intended to ensure the Pharaoh's eternity. They all reflected the opulent wealth and fortune and the refined art that was produced by the Royal court in the sumptuous times of the New Kingdom.

The statues that represent this child-King, this King-God, show him in a heavenly perfection. Draped with dignity and dressed in a costume of shimmering golden light, his eyes watch us across more than three thousand years. We see him as a king who was more triumphant after his death than during his life time... Without a single word or gesture, he seems to represent Egypt, its treasures and its civilisation. Calm and serene, as if he knew that his name would cross the centuries, despite those who profaned his memory, to continue honouring his God and transmitting his message of eternity from the kingdom of the dead.

Aly **MAHER EL SAYED**
Ambassador of Egypt

CONTENTS

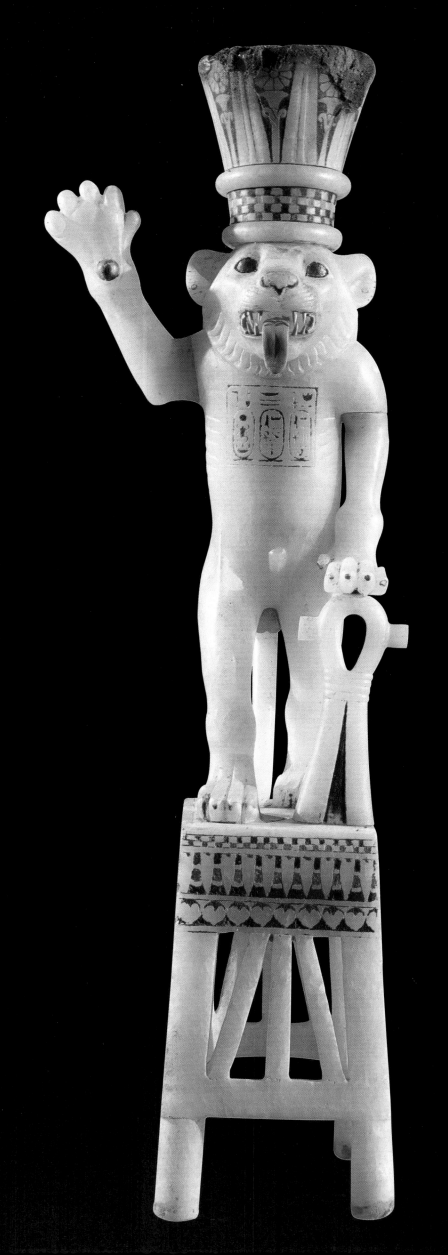

HISTORY
THE 18TH DYNASTY

Tutankhamun and his time

The history of Ancient Egypt spreads out over almost three thousand years. From the moment king *Narmer* unified the kingdom in 3150 b.c. to the conquest of *Alexander the Great*, we find an ensemble of thirty dynasties that are divided into prosperous and propitious Kingdoms and into Intermediate Periods. Some of these are partially or completely unknown and correspond to dark and uncertain eras plagued with social unrest, economic problems, political disruptions and foreign invasions. The Old Kingdom follows an interval which can not be placed with great certainty, the Early Dynastic Period. It was then that Egypt became unified under one commander, and set down the religious, political, social and administrative rules that were to be followed from then on, as were writing styles and artistic cannons. The kings established the capital in **Memphis** and the country found itself immersed in an extremely singular degree of excellence. Stone architecture begins to spring up timidly, kings chose pyramids as their burial place, whilst private individuals preferred **mastabas** in which reliefs and paintings related the scenes of everyday life in great detail.

The 6th Dynasty saw an acute drop of royal authority, which was accentuated by the ever-increasing power of the **nomarchs**. These were the provincial governors, a post that had become hereditary and, thus, had allowed for the establishment of real dynasties, which in some cases were more powerful than the Pharaoh himself. Local officials grasped their independence and Egypt seemed to be under the threat of foreign invaders. Royalty had become weakened by the long reign of *Pepy II* and could not get the situation under command. Egypt became engulfed in a period of great confusion: the First Intermediate Period. Anarchy reigned: kinglets grabbed power, the nobility was stripped of their property, lands were abandoned and poverty haunted the country.

The unification of the land under one unique commander marked the advent of the Middle Kingdom. In the fifteenth year of his reign *Mentuhotep I*, ruler of the **Theban** region, became the pharaoh of Upper and Lower Egypt. This new era of prosperity brought with it many political, administrative and religious reforms. Economic progress was made through exploiting virgin land: **Sinai**, the desert of Libya, the Arabian Desert, **Nubia** and **Fayum**. However, for reasons that are still unclear, the 12th Dynasty ended in a haze of famine, internal quarrels and foreign invasions. Therefore, it seems more than evident that the arrival of the **Hyksos**, who probably reached Egypt from Asia, is the starting point of the destabilisation of the country, which now falls into another unfortunate period: the Second Intermediary Period. The **Hyksos** reign over the North, the South and the whole country, and set up their capital at **Avaris**, in the Nile Delta. However, at the beginning of the 17th Dynasty, some princes of **Thebes** declared war against the invaders.

Ahmose inaugurates the New Kingdom and will later found the 18th Dynasty. This era is one of splendour and refinement, bringing a revival of royal power, a great territorial expansion and flow of wealth coming into Egypt. The pharaohs set up their capital in **Thebes**, "the City of the Hundred Doors", which rapidly becomes a symbol of prosperity, wealth and luxury. This is the land *Tutankhamun* reigned over. Nonetheless, the intensification of the role that religion and the clergy came to play in State affairs inevitably led to a degradation of monarchic power. The Kingdom was ruined by the successive usurpation of power and internal conflict. It was corrupt and fragile, and could no longer drive away the foreigners whose presence had become more and more insistent at Egypt's borders.

Thutmose III

Thutmose III, considered the "hero" of the dynasty, succeeded queen Hatshepsut on the Egyptian throne. Under his reign, the Kingdom spread out from the fourth cataract in Nubia in the South to the Euphrates in the East. Here we see the king represented as in the form of a bird with a human head, wearing a nemes on his head. His name is engraved on his torso and surrounded by a cartouche.

Red jasper.
The Louvre.

From Ahmose to Thutmose IV

In all likelihood, the war against the **Hyksos**, lords of the Delta and of the north of Egypt, began during the reign of *Taa II,* penultimate king of the 17th Dynasty and father of *Kamose* and *Ahmose,* who would later become the liberators of the country. However, there is a great lack of documents concerning this king. At the very most, through his mummified body, found in the cache at **Deir el-Bahri**, we know he died from wounds after receiving blows from aggressors who carried lances and war axes. He was succeeded by *Kamose,* whose main concern was chasing out the Hyksos sovereigns who inhabited **Avaris**, in the north-east of the Delta. The first confrontation between their armies ended with the victory of the Egyptian troops who then took the village of **Neferusy**, located to the north of **Hermopolis.** Then *Kamose* sailed back up the river to **Avaris** and, according to his own words, the battle concluded with the ransack of the Asian village. When *Ahmose* rose to the Egyptian throne after his brother's death he concluded the liberation of the country and, once victorious, restored the pharaonic rule, thus inaugurating both the 18th Dynasty and the New Kingdom. The account of the different campaigns carried out against the Hyksos invaders can be read on a very detailed historical inscription, carved in **El-Kab** at the entrance of the tomb of **Ahmose son of Ibana**, a nobleman who had fought in the royal army when the events took place. He notably took part in the siege and fall of the Hyksos capital: *"We took Avaris. I took some prisoners: one man and three women. His Majesty let me keep them as servants."* Once the Asians had been defeated he pursued them to Palestine where he ransacked the village of **Sharuhen.** The danger the Hyksos posed was discarded once and for all after that campaign. An administrative, economic and fiscal reorganisation came with the reconquest of the country. The provincial governors or **Nomarchs** lost all their autonomy and became part of a central administration, which was strictly controlled by the king. Dykes and irrigation channels were cleaned out and rearranged; the country continued opening-up towards the Near East, an action that was initiated in the Middle Kingdom, and wealth began to flow into Egypt once again. Quarries were reopened and the building of religious and funerary constructions was taken up again. A stele, discovered near the eighth pylon in the great temple of **Karnak** gives evidence of this newly regained prosperity. In the offering *Ahmose* prepared for *"his father Amun-Ra"* there were all types of objects made in the most precious materials: gold, silver, lapis lazuli, turquoise, ebony, cedar wood...

Regarding the military aspect, the sovereigns of the 18th Dynasty engrossed themselves in a policy of expansionism, a logical consequence of the war fought against the **Hyksos.** Thus, during the reign of *Thutmose III,* the "hero" of the dynasty, Egypt's authority could be felt from the Euphrates to the fourth cataract. A stele in **Gebel Barkal** bears the inscription: *"There are no longer rebels in the southern countries and the northern countries stoop to my glory."* An immediate consequence of this supremacy was that the coffers of the kingship, such as those belonging to *Amun* were crammed with wealth and riches that were collected from the tributes that vassal states paid to Egypt. These were most importantly the land of **Djahi** in Syria-Palestine and the land of **Retenu** in Syria in the North, and the land of **Wawat**, Lower Nubia, the land of **Kush** and Higher Nubia in the South. Foreign princes (from **Cyprus**, **Assyria**, the land of **Hatti** in Anatolia, **Babylon** and the land of **Punt** on the Somalian coast) also paid their tributes and presented many gifts hoping to gain the Pharaoh 's trust.

Many sumptuous buildings were constructed in Egypt, all dedicated to the most important divinities of the Pantheon. In **Thebes**, particularly, the temple of *Amun* continued to grow bigger and more beautiful: **Karnak** became a national sanctuary, pharaohs made never-ending donations grateful to the gods for guiding them towards victory. **West Thebes** became the necropolis of the New Kingdom par excellence. From the beginning of the 18th Dynasty *Thutmose I* introduced a radical change in the structure of the complex burial ritual: he separated the tombs, which from then on were to be situated in the **Valley of the Kings**, from the funerary temples, which were now to be situated on the outskirts of the desert. These grandiose sanctuaries, called the "Castles of A Million Years" had spacious properties and held many residences. The most important funerary divinities can be found here, but *Amun* and other great gods worshipped during the Kingdom are also present. This probably meant to associate royal and divine destiny.

Amenhotep III: the Sun King

After his death, *Thutmose IV* was succeeded by his son *Amenhotep III.* He inherited a pacific, stable and powerful kingdom, and thus never felt the need to turn to force to maintain Egyptian authority in the regions of Libya, **Nubia** and the Near East. Egypt's supremacy had reached the height of its prestige and prosperity. From then on it would be based on a subtle game of alliances with Asian countries and also with the vassal states of Syria-Palestine. These alliances were made with the hope of developing Egypt's economic power in the Mediterranean area, maintaining a strong hold on the wealth that stemmed from Africa and ensuring that commercial paths were secure. These diplomatic relations between Egypt and Asia are well documented due to the finding of a series of clay tablets in 1887. These were inscribed in cuneiform writing mostly in Akkadian, the *lingua franca* of the Near East. They were given the name of the **"Amarna** Letters", due to the region they were found in, and are made up of a assembly of three hundred and fifty tablets which date from the thirtieth year of the reign of *Amenhotep III* to the third year of *Tutankhamun's* reign, although the great majority date from the reign of **Amenhotep IV-Akhenaten.** These unique archives record the administrative and political correspondence between the sovereigns. Some record the difficulties the vassal states encountered under the invasion of countries that were Egypt's enemies; these make up a desperate cry for help addressing the king and begging him to send help to the princes of these besieged countries. Others deal with the value of precious metals or rare commodities, commercial relations, diplomatic marriages, trade... This letter written by the king of Babylon to Amenhotep III is a sound example: *"Regarding my daughter, the young lady about whom you wrote to me concerning the arrangement of a marriage, she has now become a woman: she is nubile. Simply send a party of your men to meet her and take her to you. Formerly, my father sent you a messenger whom you did not keep with you for very long; you sent him back rapidly although you also sent a beautiful present. Yet, when it was I who sent you a messenger, you kept him for six years and only sent me one thing during that time: thirty gold mines, full of a material that resembled silver more than gold! That gold was melted in the presence of your messenger Kasi, therefore he can testify to the truthfulness of the event. When you organised a party, you did not send me a messenger saying: come, eat and drink. You did not send me a tribute in connection to the party. Those thirty mines of gold have been your only gift. The present you have sent me can not be compared to what I present to you every year."*

Among the many foreign princesses he kept in his harem, *Amenhotep III* married *Tiy* to carry out the role of his main wife. She was not of Royal blood, being the daughter of **Yuya** and **Tuyu** who originated from **Ahkmim** in Upper Egypt. This queen has come to be one of the most renowned of the dynasty due to the eminent role she played during her husband's life: she is associated to the king's power and regularly appears next to the pharaoh in the statuary, on the reliefs in many temples or tombs, on stelae... In these representations, she is depicted with the iconography of the great Egyptian goddesses, most importantly Hathor wearing cow horns and her sun disc. *Amenhotep III* and *Tiy's* reign is marked by an intense architectural activity, both in Egypt and in **Nubia.** Alongside the work being carried out in **Karnak** and **Luxor** for the *Amun* sanctuaries, the king ordered the construction of a funerary temple in **West Thebes**; it was to be a grandiose temple sheltered exclusively by two imposing statues, known as the **"Colossi of Memnon"**, and a few scattered blocks. In the words of the king, there was nothing like it anywhere in the world: *"A spectacular temple was made for him... The temple is completely covered with gold, paved with silver, and all its doors are made of electrum."* The royal couple chose another site in **Malkata**, not far away from the former, to erect their palace. Temples, bark shrines, habitation places, ceremonial rooms, official chambers, attics, studios, and gardens all give testimony to the size of the royal palace. Reliefs and other objects exemplify the sophistication that surrounded the king and his court: wood or ivory make-up palettes, perfume vases and decanters in every shape and size made of the finest coloured glass, small statues of servants or protective divinities, various cosmetic items. These all gave notice of the way the king enjoyed living. Two other architectonic masterpieces of the New Kingdom can be found in **Nubia:** the temple of **Soleb**, dedicated to *Amenhotep III*, and the temple of **Sedinga**, dedicated to *Tiy.*

Royal head statue presumed to depict Amenhotep III

The king is wearing the khepresh, or war crown with round motifs, over which the uraeus has been wound. The artist has managed to give the face a very realistic expression, which has been accentuated by the trace of a smile that gives life to the sovereign's gentle features.

The Louvre.

Akhenaten: the Amarnian heresy

Amenhotep IV was the youngest son borne by queen *Tiy* and the great *Amenhotep III.* He reigned for seventeen years, during which he left a singular mark on pharaonic culture and religion by acclaiming *Aten,* the visible manifestation of the Sun, as the dynastic divinity. However, Aten was not created by *Amenhotep IV,* his name had already been recorded in the **"Pyramid Texts"**, although simply as another manifestation of the Sun God *Ra-Harakhty.* Aten had started to be worshipped in the regal years of *Thutmose IV* and *Amenhotep III,* but it was *Amenhotep IV* who brought him to the status of supreme god, who lights up the world with his beneficial rays, gives life and provides heat. The artistic representations that appear during these years depict the king and his family worshipping the sun disc with outstretched rays ending in hands that bear the ankh cross, symbol of life, that emanates from the Pharaoh. The explanation can be found in a simple sentence: *"You rise peacefully towards the Horizon, oh Aten, giver of life, but not a person knows you, only your son Akhenaten. You have laid your plans and your power before him."* The sovereign seems to have taken on the role of official mediator: he became the prophet of *Aten,* his representation on earth and the essential intermediary between the god and his subjects. Thus, no one knew how to worship *Aten* directly, only the king and his family. Ordinary men and women venerated *Akhenaten,* who in his turn venerated the sun disc himself.

There are many hypotheses that aim to explain this religious transformation: political reasons, the pharaoh's personality, the real religious foundations of this new belief… Nonetheless, with what is known today, nothing can be confirmed and, therefore, none of these assumptions are truly convincing. It is most probable that a combination of many factors led to this heresy: the new king aimed to limit the power of the clergy of *Amun;* he honestly wished to honour the sun in its most dazzling manifestation: the disc; his personality was quite ambiguous and philosophical, he was a thinker but he was also mythical and even fanatical at times. However it may be, at some time between the fourth and eighth year of his reign, *Amenhotep IV* broke off all associations with the clergy of Amun and left **Thebes** for **Akhetaten**, "The Horizon of *Aten*" or "The Horizon of the Sun Disc" (a land which today is known as **Tell el Amarna**). The name of the old dynastic god was banished as was the word "god" used in its plural form, as the pharaoh only recognised one god: *Aten.* He also changed his name from *Amenhotep* (meaning, *"Amun* is satisfied") to *Akhenaten* (meaning "Glory of *Aten"*). During this Amarnian period, a radical modification of Egyptian artistic cannons took place alongside the religious turn. The idealism that was the trend during the 18th Dynasty is now abandoned in favour of a striking realism that at times verges on caricature. The representations depict images whose heads are pushed backwards unnaturally, equine faces, thin almond-shaped eyes, extremely long ears, large nose, protruding chin, thin neck, small chest, slim waist, spindly extremities, womanly breasts, round stomach and swollen hips. The king adopts truly androgynous forms, although the reasons for imposing these unusual artistic cannons remain unknown.

The last three years of the Amarnian period are surrounded by controversy due to the appearance of an enigmatic person: *Smenkhkara.* His links to the royal family are unfamiliar: he could have been a younger brother of *Akhenaten,* an older brother or a half brother of *Tutankhamun…* It seems he was summoned by the pharaoh himself, who granted him princess *Meritaten,* his eldest daughter, as his wife. He then became his associate to the throne and they ruled together. Yet, two years after those events took place, *Smenkhkara* and *Akhenaten* passed away within months of each other. The royalty then chose *Tutankhamun* to succeed him. He was only nine years old. *Akhenaten's* tomb was discovered at the beginning of the Twentieth Century in the cliffs to the east of **Akhetaten**. At first some archaeologist believed that, due to the investigations carried out in situ, the burial chamber seemed to have been sealed at the moment of the funeral. Others disagreed with this statement due to the deplorable state the objects were found in, both in the tomb and surrounding it. Everything had been smashed to smithereens. In fact, if *Akhenaten* was brought here at first, he could not have been left here long. When the village was abandoned, his partisans most probably moved his body, but where ? It could have been to the **Valley of Kings** but it could have been elsewhere. His bearings are still unknown as his mummy is still to be discovered

Amenhotep IV

Many statues of Amenhotep IV have been found. They mainly come from The Temple of Aten in Karnak, a sanctuary the king had arranged for himself before deciding to set up the capital in Tell el Amarna. This statue probably dates from the beginning of his reign, the Amarnian cannons already heavily influencing it: almond shaped eyes, prominent chin…

The Cairo Museum.

Tutankhamun's reign

Surprising though it may seem, *Tutankhamun* is still a mysterious character of the end of the 18th Dynasty, and unfortunately, the discovery of his tomb has not unveiled many things about him or the historical context of his era. His parentage is still mostly unknown; however, one thing is certain: he is the son of a king, as read on an inscription found in **Hermopolis.** However, one cannot clearly state his direct ancestors. Some consider he is the son of wealthy *Amenhotep III* and queen *Tiy*: this theory relies on a series of documents showing that the official policy during the young king's reign was to give credence to that connection. Others believe he is the son of *Amenhotep IV* and *Kiya*, whose true identity is not clear either, although it is known that she was the princess of **Tadugepha,** daughter of **Tushratta,** king of **Mitanni.** *Tutankhamun's* place of birth has also given rise to a certain degree of controversy: **Thebes** or **Akhetaten?** One thing is certain: whether or not he was born in **Akhetaten,** he was certainly raised there, in the capital *Akhenaten* created to honour *Aten,* as he initially bore the name *Tutanhkaten,* "the living image of Aten".

He was still a nine-year-old child when he came to the throne, and he was already married to *Ankhesenpaaten, Akhenaten's* third daughter. Obviously, although *Tutankhamun* was the king, he did not rule the country himself. Two people shared the power: *Ay,* the God's Father, and general *Horemheb.* The fact remains that from the beginning of his regal years, the religion was reverted back to the worship of *Amun,* the true god of the Kingdom. The measures undertaken by the king in order to restore the ancient belief that prevailed in Egypt under *Amenhotep III* are inscribed on the stele of the "Restoration of the Theban temples", which was to be placed in the north-eastern corner of the great hypostyle room in **Karnak.** This stele, which was appropriated by *Horemheb* (probably its true author), supposes a radical change in the history of the New Kingdom, and puts an end to the Amarnian heresy. Due to this reform the king changed his name and removed any traces of *Aten* : in the second year of his being in power he abandoned *Tutankhaten* and became *Tutankhamun,* "Living image of *Amun".* His wife also took on a new name: from *Ankhesenpaaten* she became *Ankhesenamun.*

During the first years, the couple most probably lived in **Malkata (West Thebes),** in the sumptuous residence that had belonged to *Amenhotep III.* However, it is more than likely that the official residence was later taken to **Memphis.** It is quite difficult to pinpoint any events that took place during *Tutankhamun's* reign other than the restoration of the belief in *Amun* and the restoration of the temples of the Theban Triad. Some reliefs that have been found in **Karnak** and **Luxor** evoke military campaigns in Asia and **Nubia.** Even though these incidents have been confirmed by representations found in both *Horemheb's* tomb in **Saqqara** and **Huy's** tomb in **Thebes,** it is unthinkable that the young king took part in either of them. *Ay* and *Horemheb* are not the only important individuals in times of *Tutankhamun,* other dignitaries also surrounded the king. **Maya** was *"Director of all the works in the Place of Truth",* at the royal necropolis, and *"Treasury official".* He was in charge of *Tutankhamun's* funeral and placed a recumbent effigy and a **shabti** bearing his name in the sepulchre. He is also renowned through the splendid reliefs discovered on his tomb in 1843 in **Saqqara** near *Horemheb's* first tomb, which was forgotten and then found again in 1986. **Nakhtmin** was also fortunate enough to leave five big **shabtis** in the king's vault. But who was he? He must have been an officer of the army, a close relative of *Ay,* the "God's Father". Had he wanted, as many have said, to become *Ay's* successor to the Egyptian throne? This remains unconfirmed. As for **Huy,** he was buried in tomb n°. 40 in **West Thebes** and as the *"Viceroy of Kush"* he was in charge of defending Egyptian interests in Nubian lands.

Tutankhamun passed away after a short-lived and not very prestigious reign, unquestionably influenced by *Ay* and *Horemheb.* Maybe he did not have the ability to impose his wishes. A difficult political context, along with rising to the throne at such an early age, his frail health and a premature death all stopped him from becoming a glorious pharaoh. He died in the ninth year of his reign, when he was approximately nineteen years old, in strange circumstances. His mummy was found with a wound in the left cranial cavity. Was that the cause of his death? If so, was it an accident, a fall or was he assassinated? Unfortunately, all these questions remain unanswered.

Tutankhamun depicted as the god Amun

In this grandiose statue erected on the walls that surround the temple of Karnak, in the territory of Amun, god of the New Kingdom, Tutankhamun is depicted with the dynastic god's features and attributes: he is wearing the double-feathered high crown and the godly long thin false beard, a divine feature.

Karnak Temple, East Thebes.

Page 23

Tutankhamun depicted as the god Khons

This statue was found in the great temple dedicated to Amun in Karnak.. The young pharaoh is depicted as Kohns, the child god of the Theban Triad, son of Amun and Mut. He wears the sidelock of youth, trait of young children, and the royal insignia of the uraeus on his forehead.

Black granite.
The Cairo Museum.

FAMILY TREE

Tutankhamun, son of Amenhotep III

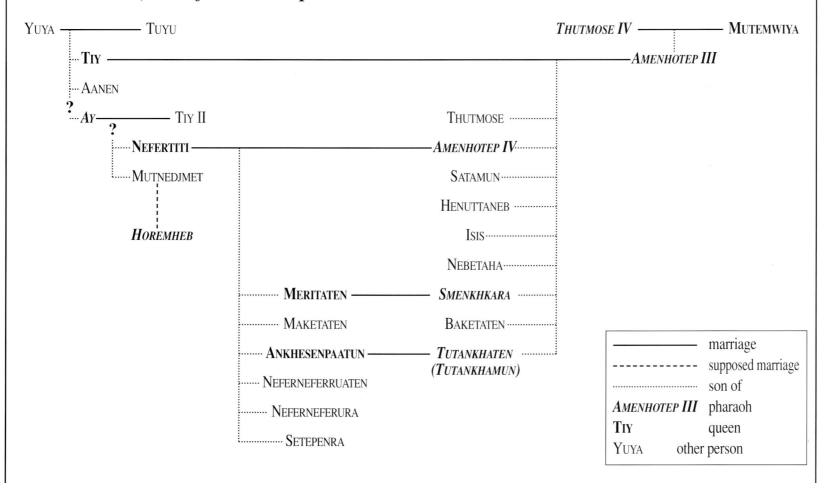

Legend:

——————	marriage
- - - - - - -	supposed marriage
··············	son of
AMENHOTEP III	pharaoh
TIY	queen
YUYA	other person

Tutankhamun, son of Amenhotep IV

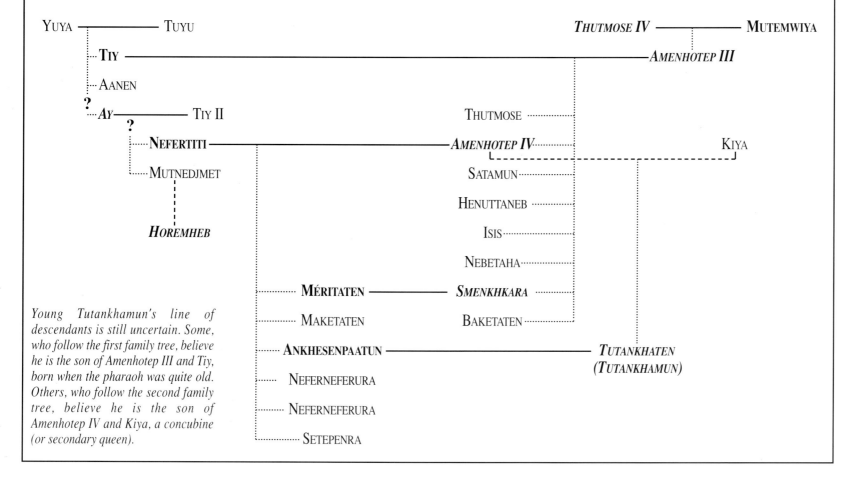

Young Tutankhamun's line of descendants is still uncertain. Some, who follow the first family tree, believe he is the son of Amenhotep III and Tiy, born when the pharaoh was quite old. Others, who follow the second family tree, believe he is the son of Amenhotep IV and Kiya, a concubine (or secondary queen).

The end of the 18th Dynasty

Tutankhamun's premature death, leaving behind no male heir to the throne posed a difficult problem: the line of succession. Among those close to him, one man stands out, a man who has played an extremely important role in the nucleus of the government: *Ay*, the God's Father, the king's main adviser. Today he is still an enigmatic character. At the most, it is known that *Amenhotep IV-Akhenaten* already considered him a trustworthy man. He must have exerted a considerable influence over the young king, and according to some historians, he may even have "chosen" himself as co-regent. However it may have been, *Ay* succeeded *Tutankhamun* on the Egyptian throne, and so as to legitimise his power, he married *Ankhesenamun*, the deceased pharaoh's widow. A ring can confirm this wedlock: they are both represented on the setting, their names appear set next to each other on a cartouche. Nonetheless, the "God's Father" was already quite old when he rose to the throne, and after a four year reign, he passed away and was given a royal funeral. He was buried in a tomb that had initially been prepared for *Tutankhamun* and was located in the **Valley of the Monkeys,** to the west of the **Valley of the Kings.** Not many documents have survived that ephemeral reign, most probably because *Horemheb* (who then succeeded Ay) did his best to erase him from memory.

Originally from Middle Egypt, *Horemheb* first appears during *Akhenaten's* reign. Then he was just a royal scribe, known as **Paatonemheb.** He quickly rose to the position of generalissimo and installed himself in **Memphis.** During *Tutankhamun's* years in power he was one of the most important persons in the country. He was awarded the title of "Prince", which granted him more power than the viziers. A vast funerary monument he built in the **Saqqara** necropolis, near the *Unas* pyramid, dates from that period. This tomb, which was discovered in the Nineteenth Century by the German archaeologist *Richard Lepsius*, totally stripped of all its statues and reliefs which were taken to Western museums or private collections. Then it was left to the sands of the desert, and fell into oblivion. After a detailed study was carried out on remaining fragments that had been collected in the Western museums, an archaeological mission was undertaken in 1975 on that part of the **Saqqara** plateau. It was then that *Horemheb's* lost sepulchre was found once again.

The excavations have determined that this tomb had been used to bury the body of queen *Mutnedjmet*, and has been executed exquisitely. She was probably one of *Nefertiti's* sisters, whom *Horemheb* wedded to legitimise his power and create a link with the reigning dynasty. Thus, after *Ay's* death, *Horemheb* became the new Egyptian king. He was crowned in **Karnak,** during a New Year celebration: *"I was established king, and the god inclined his head: we were face to face before the whole world. The command came from heaven and was heard in Karnak. The Ennead was in celebration."* And *Amun* said: *"You are my son and I have placed you on my throne, as master and regent of all that surrounds the disk. You are Horemheb, Amun-Ra's beloved, Master of the thrones of the Double-Country, and you preside over Karnak."* The first matter was to reorganise the kingdom, that was saturated with ambitious and dishonest officials who had become independent due to the trouble the Amarnian schism produced. **Horemheb** put forth his reform program by decree. The introduction is very eloquent: *"His Majesty has pondered with all his heart to establish his protection over the country as a whole, drive out evil and destroy lies... He has stayed up days and nights trying to determine what this much-loved country needs. He searched for beneficial actions... He himself has issued the decree that has been sealed by his Majesty, so as to put an end to the acts of banditry that have been occurring in this country."* The measures he lay forth were supposed to prevent plundering and robberies, to protect the people, forbid the abusive requisitioning of countrymen, and to prevent all corruption in the administration. *Horemheb* also pursued the restoration of the worship of *Amun*, that began during *Tutankhamun's* reign. In **Karnak** he accomplished or started the second, the ninth and the tenth pylons: all three of these are made up by two massive blocks of stone packed with small crudely fashioned blocks called **talatat** blocks, originally from temples that were dedicated to *Aten*. Horemheb died after thirty years of power, leaving behind him a powerful and respected land. He was finally buried in the **Valley of the Kings,** given that, from the moment he was crowned, he decided to stop the work that was being carried out on his funerary monument in **Saqqara,** and he chose to be buried in a vault reserved for the Egyptian pharaohs; one of the most beautiful hypogeums in **West Thebes.**

Horemheb

Horemheb's tomb can be found to the north-west of the Valley of the Kings and is still one of the best kept sepulchres of the Theban necropolis. The figures and inscription still bear great traces of colour. They come away from the grey-blue background which makes the representation more delicate than ever. Here Horemheb is depicted before the divinities of the Netherworld. Goddess Isis is behind him, wearing the crown usually worn by Hathor, although she can be recognised as her name is inscribed above her head.

Tomb nº. 57.
Valley of the Kings,
West Thebes.

THE DISCOVERY
AN INTACT SEPULCHRE...

West Thebes during the New Kingdom

Thutmose I introduced a radical modification in the organisation of the funerary structure used in Egypt. He separated sepulchres, located in the **Valley of the Kings**, from funerary temples, which he built on the outskirts of the desert. On the Nile's left bank, directly below the Theban Peak, we find "the Great Place", the necropolis built for the pharaohs of the New Kingdom. It is divided into two distinguishable wadis: to the West, the **Valley of the Monkeys** which houses four tombs including *Amenhotep III* and *Ay*, the God's Father. To the East, the **Valley of the Kings**, or **Biban el Moluk** in Arabian, meaning the "Doors of the Kings", housing fifty-eight tombs from the 18th, 19th and 20th Dynasties. Some tombs are just excavations cluttered with rubble, whereas others still enclose the secrets of luxurious funerals, even if the funerary treasures are no longer found within. Although these sepulchres were initially kept in secrecy, *"no one sees, no one hears"* the saying went, they soon attracted tomb plunderers.

The first robberies took place under the reign of *Ramesses IX*, during the 20th Dynasty, they were deemed insignificant and, according to the records, were seemingly ignored by the inspectors or the officials in charge of watching over the necropolis in **West Thebes**. However, barely a few decades later, this time under *Ramesses XI*, the ransacking was carried out with greater determination. During the 21st Dynasty, *Pinudjem* ordered the inspection of the vaults, so as to save whatever the plunderers had not taken and restore any mummified bodies that had been damaged in the deed. They stored all the mummies together in two caches: one part was hidden in the tomb of *Amenhotep II*, and another part in a cache hidden in a cliff near **Deir el-Bahri** (the royal mummies of *Amenhotep I*, *Thutmose III*, *Sety I*, *Ramesses II*, among others, were concealed here). Most vaults were identical in their general disposition: a door cut vertically in the rock, a long corridor with many continuous narrow sections flanked by niches or lateral shrines, and one or two burial chambers. Sometimes the

tombs were more than 328 feet long. The most eye-catching elements are the decorations carved or painted on the rock face: hundreds of figures, fitted tightly together, winding all the way around the sepulchre. Although the images that depict the life of the deceased and his funerary service are represented inside the funerary temple, the walls of the tomb itself are reserved for manifestations that represent all that concerns the journey of the soul to the infernal world. These documents, be they partially or entirely written in a figurative sense, are gathered in the funerary books that were compiled in more or less ancient times.

"**The Litany of Ra**" describes *Ra*, the Sun god, relating his qualities, his purpose, his symbols, his nature and his different manifestations (approximately seventy-five), all of which should be known by the king in order for him to identify himself with the god. The "**Book of the Opening of the Mouth**" relates the rituals that can grant the pharaoh's mummified body and the statue of the Double the power to receive offerings and to feed on them. The "**Book of that which is in the Netherworld**" and the "**Book of Gates**" are two different versions of the same notion: identification of the king with the god *Ra*. This other world is divided into twelve domains which are all washed by the infernal Nile whose banks are inhabited by strange genii that symbolise all the evils the human body can experience, thus the representation of reptiles armed with pikes and knives. The sun boat sails along the river carrying *Ra* and other divinities: *Hathor*, the patron of the crew, the jackal *Apuiau* who guides the way along the infernal pathways, *Horus* the crier, the Double of *Shu*, *Hu* the sailor, *Sa* the pilot; the guardian and the captain. In certain areas, legends quote the name of the domain, the name of the Hour of the Night who dwells there, the name of his or her guardian, the true scope of his or her territory, the names of the genii or gods that can be found there, and the words the fallen Sun pronounced upon entering said territory: he who knows all these names and all these words can join the Sun.

Canopic jar lid

This marvellous object was found in tomb n°. 55 of the Valley of the Kings, it has still not been correctly identified as it is unmarked. Many objects have been found in this anonymous tomb, most importantly a gilt wood shrine, a mummy laying in its coffin, some figurines and four Canopic Jars, one of which was closed with this lid. The last studies carried out on the mummy have led to believe the occupant was Smenkhkara, princess Meritaten's husband, who co-reigned with Akhenaten for two years.

Calcite.
Tomb n°. 55.
The Cairo Museum.

The first signs of Tutankhamun

Theodore Davis was in charge of the **Valley of the Kings** in the early Twentieth Century. He was a rich retired American lawyer, who had started studying the area in 1902, first through works directed by **Howard Carter**, then the General Inspector of Upper Egyptian monuments, and then by a series of free-lance archaeologists. In 1914, after unveiling around 30 tombs, some more interesting than others, **Davis** discovered the first traces of *Tutankhamun's* name on three occasions. A small blue faience cup with the young king's cartouche stamped on it was found in the winter of 1906, 49 feet to the East of **Amenemopet's** tomb (private tomb n°. 48), in a cache found at the foot of a rock. In all likelihood, plunderers brought it out of the sepulchre thinking it was made of glass, a material that was greatly sought-after during the 18th Dynasty.

In the following year, 1907, archaeologists spotted an irregular cache hidden in the side of a rock: well n°. 54, which was about 5 feet deep. A very superficial analysis revealed that it was full of strips of linen, pieces of pottery and debris. **Davis** deemed the find totally uninteresting, thus he stored it in his house and forgot about it. It was there that **Herbert Winlock** (from **The Metropolitan Museum of Art**), noticed them on his way to **West Thebes** and asked for **Davis'** permission to send them to New York for a more in-depth analysis. After this second analysis, experts came to the conclusion that the well contained the remnants of the embalming process of young *Tutankhamun's* body, alongside the remains of his funerary banquet. Large terracotta jars are amongst the most interesting objects found in the collection. Some were still plugged with a stopper bearing the seal of the royal necropolis (the jackal Anubis dominating nine captives) and the name of *Tutankhamun*, the beloved of many a god, *Ptah* and *Knum* among others. It also contained some rags of linen shawls that bore inscriptions written in hieratic lettering referring to the sixth and eighth year of the young king's reign.

The rest of the findings were unmarked, but extremely interesting nonetheless: small strips with selvages woven specially for the bandaging of the body; packets of linen full of natron, a sodium carbonate used in mummification processes, linen fabric (notably three semicircular handkerchiefs which were most certainly used as wig-holders), sachets of a powdery material that constitute the waste left over from the embalming process, some bones and some pieces of pottery. Among the decorations: ruffles of blue faience beads and flowers sewn on a papyrus support, an ornament worn by guests during funerals, and a small golden cartonnage mask probably made for the oldest foetus found in the **Treasury** in *Tutankhamun's* tomb. There is a link between these objects and the burying of the young pharaoh. According to **Winlock**, during funerary rituals these objects were placed in the passage that led to the sepulchre, which was probably then empty. After the first robbery, officials had most probably decided to block up the passage, hoping to impede future plunderers accessing the subterranean chambers, and decided to transport all that material to well n°. 54.

In 1909, **Harold James**, one of **Davis'** workers, entered a seemingly insignificant and undecorated subterranean chamber: room n°. 58, located slightly to the north of *Horemheb's* tomb, 24 feet under ground. It contained a beautiful alabaster **shabti** that could have belonged to *Ay*, the God's Father, and a small broken wooden box which contained fragments of sheets of gold that bore the figures of *Tutankhamun* and his wife *Ankhesenamun*. Linking these three discoveries, **Davis** and his collaborators inferred they were on the verge of finding *Tutankhamun's* tomb. However, they thought it had suffered the same fate as the royal hypogeums that surrounded it: it had been ransacked by plunderers in the Ramesside period. Having reached that conclusion, **Davis** gave up on the searches being carried out in the **Valley of the Kings**; the preface to the book he wrote describing his latest excavations quotes: *"I fear that the Valley of the Kings is now exhausted."* Yet, after carrying out a meticulous analysis of all the objects that had been discovered by **Davis'** team, **Howard Carter** noted that they all had one thing in common: most of them related either to the mummification ritual, or to the funerary banquet that was served after the burial near the sepulchre. In any case, there is no trace of the actual funerary material. Thus, nothing denotes that well n°. 54 and room n°. 58 do not contain all of *Tutankhamun's* remains.

THE VALLEY OF THE KINGS

The "Great Place" is located on the Nile's left bank, directly below the Theban Peak, constituting the necropolis used by the kings of the New Kingdom. It consists of two distinguishable wadis: to the West, the **Valley of the Monkeys**, that houses four tombs (nos. 22 to 25) including those of *Amenhotep III* and *Ay*, the God's Father. To the East, the actual **Valley of the Kings**, or **Biban el Moluk** in Arabic, meaning the "Doors of the Kings", housing fifty-eight tombs (nos. 1 to 21, and from n°. 26 to 62) bearing most of the pharaohs of the 18th, 19th and 20th Dynasties. Of the sixty-two listed tombs, some are unmarked and anonymous, and thus are of no real interest. Others, however, were made for high ranking officials or members of the royal family (**Yuya** and **Tuyu,** queen *Tiy's* parents, **Montuherkhepeshef,** a prince who lived in the late 20th Dynasty, or **Bai**, the vizier of *Siptah* during the 19th Dynasty…). This map shows the central part of the Western wadi. Situated in the centre of the necropolis is tomb n°. 62, *Tutankhamun's* tomb, pharaoh of the late 18th Dynasty, discovered by **Howard Carter** on the 5th of November 1922.

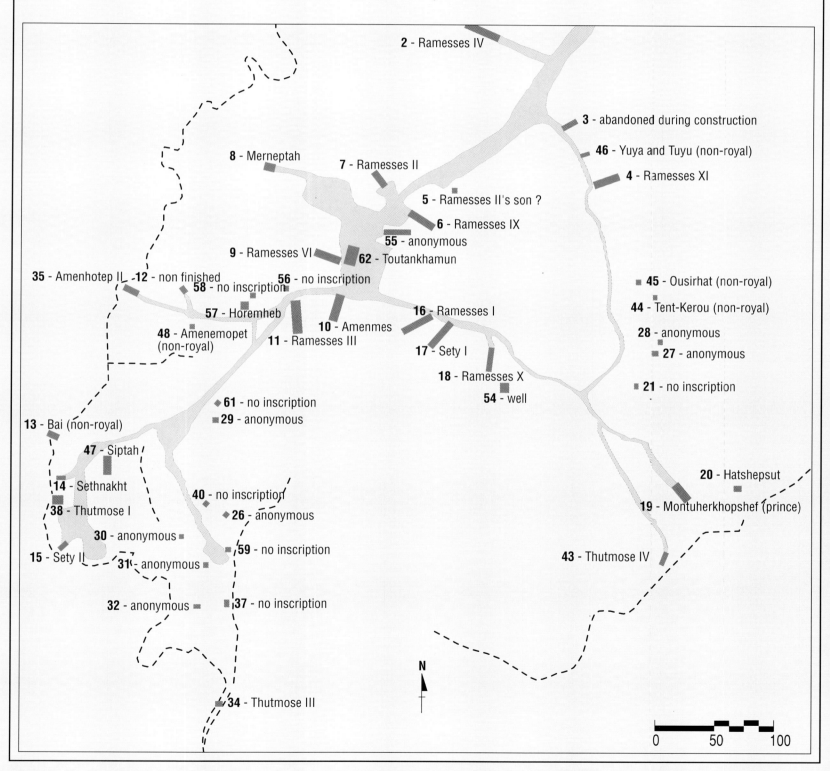

Howard Carter

Howard Carter was born in London on the 9th of May 1874, the youngest of eleven children. He came from a modest family, and although his father was a relatively renowned wildlife artist and illustrator, he only received basic schooling. Nonetheless, from a very early age he showed a great artistic gift. He was introduced to **Percy Newberry** when he was seventeen; **Newberry**, a young Egyptologist of the Egypt Exploration Found, was so impressed with his artistic talent that he hired him to make ink reproductions of the drawings copied from the private tombs of **Beni Hasan**. After this short job, he travelled to Egypt, and was immediately captivated by the country. His first experiences with archaeology were not extremely encouraging, particularly the one that took him to **Tell el-Amarna** alongside **Flinders Petrie**. The latter, not at all satisfied with his capacity to become an Egyptologist, dismissed him straight away. However, he was called upon once again by the Egypt Exploration Found, and was sent to **Thebes** as a draughtsman. Here, for six years, he copied the inscriptions on the funerary temple of queen *Hatshepsut* in **Deir el- Bahri**.

The precision and care with which he carried out his work were seemingly good assets and they caught **Gaston Maspero's** eye. Thus, he named **Carter** General Inspector of Upper Egyptian monuments, a position he took up in January 1900. During his mandate his most important mission was the clearing of various sepulchres that had recently been discovered in the Theban necropolis by the Antiquities Service and by American Egyptologist **Theodore Davis**. He performed this enterprise with such efficiency that he was transferred to **Saqqara** in 1904; however, a few months later he handed in his resignation after an unfortunate incident and gave up his public position. What had happened? Different witnesses lay the blame on a clash **Carter** had with a group of Frenchmen who intended to go into the **Serapeum.** The Frenchmen did not have an entry ticket, thus the guards did not allow them to enter the catacombs. After a few minutes, one part of the group agreed to paying the fee, the other part refused flatly to do so. Then the visitors, some with and some without tickets, forced their way into the passage and reached the dim subterranean galleries. They came out soon enough, and on realising none of the workers would lend them any candles, they demanded to be reimbursed.

Carter stepped in at this moment, having been called by the guards to put an end to the quarrel. The situation is clear: not only did the archaeologist refuse to reimburse a single penny, he also ordered the Frenchmen to leave. Their voices rose a pitch higher and they began to shout. The tourists finally left, but in full knowledge of their rights, they made a complaint about **Carter** to **Lord**

Official meeting

Carter explains the work he is carrying out in Tutankhamun's tomb to two important Egyptians.

Cromer, the British Consul General. **Lord Cromer** asked **Carter** to apologise to the competent diplomats, but by way of an apology he handed in his resignation, despite the interventions of **Maspero** and those who had taken his side: a new life started for **Carter.** He moved to **Luxor,** and earned a living mainly by painting watercolours, which he would sell to tourists at a reasonable price, and acting as a broker of pharaonic antiquities for institutions or private collections. Although he could earn a living on these activities, **Carter** was not satisfied: he dreamt of being an Egyptologist, and found himself taking giant size steps away from it! Fortunately, in 1907, he made an acquaintance that would be truly significant: he met **Lord Carnarvon.**

31

Lord Carnarvon comes into the picture

Carter, Lord Carnarvon and Callender

The three protagonists of the discovery of Tutankhamun's treasure debate a matter. Howard Carter, the discoverer, Lord Carnarvon, the sponsor and Arthur Callender, who had studied architecture, and was a good friend and assistant to Carter during the inventory processes performed as from November 1922.

The "mannequin" rises from the tomb…

Under Carter's attentive gaze, the King's Mannequin (nº. 116), found in the Antechamber near the dismantled chariots, makes its first official outing (see pages 64-65).

When the fiftieth in the line of **Carnarvon** lords set foot on Egyptian ground for the first time, nobody could have guessed how much that journey would change his life. Actually, nothing incited this wealthy man towards archaeology and even less towards Egyptology. He had travelled to Egypt only for medical reasons: after a serious car crash in 1901 he had received doctors orders to leave England for a certain time, as its cold and damp climate was now harmful for him. The doctor recommended a region situated in an area more indicated for his delicate health. Thus, **Lord Carnarvon** arrived in Cairo in 1903, and although the climate did his health a world of good, he found he had too much spare time and, therefore, decided to take up archaeology to make these interminable days shorter. He consulted **Lord Cromer** who proposed he could subsidise excavations and gained permission for him to work in the Theban necropolis, in **Sheik Abd el-Qurna**. The first results he obtained from these searches were fairly disheartening: after six weeks of work, **Lord Carnarvon**, who directed the works himself, had found nothing but a mummified cat in a wooden sarcophagus…

He attributed this bad luck to his lack of experience in the world of archaeology and did not become discouraged. Instead he went back to **Lord Cromer** once again, hoping he could gain a concession in a region less exploited than **Sheik Abd el-Qurna**. In a letter he stated that if he were granted this permission, he would address a *"scholarly man"* to carry out these works: this man was to be no other than **Howard Carter**. One last problem remained unsolved: the matter of finance. **Lord Carnarvon** had seen how costly it was to carry out a season of archaeological searches, however, **Carter** presented him with the solution, proposing that *"part of the costs would be covered by purchasing antique objects in the bazaar in Cairo or elsewhere, and then reselling them to collectors, thus obtaining a considerable profit."*

Initially the two men concentrated their efforts on the western bank of **Thebes**. The results they obtained were very encouraging, and appeared in *Five Years' Explorations in Thebes, a record of work done, 1907-1911*. Among their discoveries, the most important find was the famous **"Carnarvon tablet nº. 1"** which on one of its sides bears the inscription of *Kamose* expelling the **Hyksos**. In 1912, **Carter** and **Lord Carnarvon** planned to expand their field of research, and made their way to the Nile Delta, in **Sakha**, near **Sais**, but after fifteen days of work they were chased out by *"an invasion of vipers and cerasts that had infested the region."* After that experience, they tried their luck in **Dahshur** and in **Tell el-Balamun**, which also produced inadequate results. **Lord Carnarvon** returned to England, **Carter,** on the other hand, returned to **Luxor** with the firm intention of carrying out some work in the royal necropolis. He encountered a small obstacle: **Theodore Davis** was still in possession of the concession for the **Valley of the Kings; Lord Carnarvon** swore he *"would never speak a word to that individual again."* However, in 1914, **Carter** decided to search on his own, and discovered the tomb of *Amenhotep I*, that had been plundered in ancient times. During the following year, just before his death, **Davis** abandoned the concession, believing that nothing else could be found in that Valley. Thus **Carter** and **Lord Carnarvon** could finally commence their own excavations. They started in the **Valley of the Monkeys**, studying the tomb of *Amenhotep III*, and as from 1917, they concentrated their efforts on the **Valley of the Kings**, searching for the tomb of a specific pharaoh: *Tutankhamun*.

The discovery

"It was our last winter in the Valley. We had spent six full seasons there, working for months, to no avail, and it is not hard to imagine how disappointing and depressing it was. We had almost given up and started packing to leave the Valley in an attempt to try our luck elsewhere". These were **Howard Carter's** feelings at the end of the 1921-1922 season. Indeed, one must note that apart from a few interesting discoveries, the results were still disappointing: was **Theodore Davis** right, had the **Valley of the Kings** really been exhausted?

Thus, after drawing up the balance of the work accomplished during these six years, **Lord Carnarvon** decided to abandon the idea of hounding out any finds in the royal necropolis. In his opinion the amount of money put into the enterprise was excessively high, considering the results they had found and the unlikely chances of making a grand discovery. He informed **Carter** who obviously understood the earl's position, but given that there were still some virgin areas, he opposed leaving the Valley until he had explored them. So he asked **Lord Carnarvon**, who held the concession in name and title, for his permission to work on the site for another season; stating that he would pay all costs and that if any object were discovered by chance, it would belong to **Lord Carnarvon** by right. The earl did not know what to say, but touched by this persistence, he finally gave in: he would allow one last season, at Carter's own expenses.

Carter arrived in **Luxor** on the 28th of October 1922, and after a few days of preparation, he was ready to recommence work where he had left it the year before: to the north-east of the tomb of *Ramesses VI*. This area was covered with the ruins of huts used by the workmen who had dug out the Ramesside vault. The working program was clear: they must evacuate the habitation area, dismantle the huts and search the ground under them. By the night of the 3rd of November this had been done: a great number of sheds had been moved, and a sufficiently big area had been demarcated, allowing for the real excavations to begin. **Carter** recounts: *"The next morning, on the 4th of November, when I arrived at the site, an unusual silence made me realise that something out of the ordinary had happened. I was informed that a step cut in the rock had been discovered underneath the very first hut to be moved. It seemed too good to be true... I almost*

dared to believe we had found a tomb at last." What had just appeared before the archaeologist's eyes was undoubtedly the first step of a hidden stairway. Nonetheless, a question hovered over them: although in a necropolis a stairway could only lead to a sepulchre, this did not mean the sepulchre would be intact, whole or even finished. It could even be just an outline... The team worked frantically, and the following day just after midday, when the twelfth step had been uncovered, **Carter** caught a glimpse of the top part of a door that had been blocked, plastered, covered with the seal of the royal necropolis: *Anubis* and the nine captives of Egypt. He reached two conclusions straight away: if the Ramesside workmen had installed their huts over the entrance of the

The Antechamber

The photographs of the work were carried out at two different times: first preliminary views of the room were taken documenting the state it was found in. Then with close or long shots, the same images were photographed again, including the batch or catalogue number placed by each object. This photograph shows the northern part of the Antechamber's western wing, with the lion-headed funerary bed (n°.35), the portable chest (n°.32) and the gilt chest (n°. 44).

tomb, it must have already been hidden in that period, thus it could not have been opened since the 20th Dynasty; and if the vault had been sealed with the impression of these stamps, it must belong to a very important person.

"What a thrilling moment for an archaeologist! Alone save for my workmen, I found myself on the threshold of what might prove to be an important discovery. The passage could lead to practically anything, and I needed all my self-control to keep from battering down the door there and then…", these are **Carter's** own words. Batter down the door… He could not, he must wait for **Lord Carnarvon** who was still in England. He gave order to reseal the stairway until his arrival. The following day **Carter** sent him a telegram:

"At last have made wonderful discovery in Valley. A magnificent tomb with seals intact; closed up until your arrival; congratulations!" The answer came immediately, on the 8th of November, **Lord Carnarvon** sent two messages: *"Possibly come soon"*, and then *"Arriving in Alexandria on the 20th."*

The 23rd of November marked the day **Carter** had been waiting for: **Lord Carnarvon** and his daughter, **Lady Evelyn Herbert**, arrived in **Luxor** by train. Everything was ready at last, and the tomb could now be opened. The steps were cleared once more, and the sealed door appeared before them: *"On the lower part the seal impressions were more legible and we could clearly make out the name of **Tutankhamun**."*

Tomb nº. 62 of the Valley of the Kings

By just looking at the plans of great royal hypogeums, one can observe that the tomb of young *Tutankhamun*, nº. 62 in the **Valley of the Kings,** did not follow the model of traditional royal tombs. The tombs of *Sety I* and *Ramesses III* are exquisite examples of this type of royal sepulchre: a small door cut vertically into the rock leads to a long passage with different narrow sections, usually flanked by side-shrines or secondary niches, opening out to the burial chamber. The tombs are sometimes more than 328 feet long.

Tutankhamun's is a completely different type of sepulchre. The vault seems to be a simple private sepulchre, resembling the one of **Yuya** and **Tuyu,** queen *Tiy's* parent's (nº.46, to the west of the **Valley of the Kings"**), or tomb nº. 55 which is anonymous. It seems that the young pharaoh was not buried in the vault that was originally intended for him. The digging works for his own tomb had probably only just begun when the king died, aged barely twenty years old. Thus, the only tomb in the Valley that was sufficiently evolved was that of *Ay*, the God's Father, the king's first councillor. So as to make it serviceable for *Tutankhamun's* funeral, it was rapidly and rudimentarily adapted to the demands of a royal tomb.

When **Carter** set foot on the step that led to the tomb for the first time he noted it had been designed in a very particular manner: the first ten steps were cut into the rock, whilst the last six were made with stones that had been plastered together. Most probably, the whole staircase had been initially cut into the rock, however, as objects had to be carried into the sepulchre during the funeral, the workmen realised that the cumbersome furniture could not be deposited there undamaged, especially the shrines and the coffins which were to be placed in the **Burial Chamber.** They had to find a hasty solution: the king's burial could not be put aside. The workmen decided to take away the last six steps of the stairway, as well as the sidewalls and the lintel of the door separating the corridor from the stairway. Then, once all the objects had been placed inside the vault, all the elements were built up once again, the steps and the sidewalls were made of stone and the lintel was made of wood.There was a rudimentarily closed door at the bottom of the stairway, coated in plaster and covered

with the impression of a series of seals: some remained from the time the tomb was sealed originally, others had been applied after robberies had taken place. This entrance gave way to a long downward-sloping passageway, which had been totally covered in rubble during the discovery and sealed at the other end by another door, identical to the former one. It led to the biggest room in the tomb, it had a north-south orientation and lacked any inscriptions or frescoes. **Carter** called it the **Antechamber** because, from what he could deduce from his earlier work in the **Valley of the Kings**, the material contained within was very similar to that which was stored in the room or rooms that would precede a burial chamber in a grandiose royal hypogeum.

A low door built into the left wall of the **Antechamber** led to a smaller room, also facing north-south, where the floor was about 3 feet lower. **Carter** named this room the **Annexe**, because he thought it corresponded to the rooms that are part of burial chambers in traditional royal sepulchres.

At the far end of the **Antechamber**, on the northern side, *"there was a tempting sealed door."* It was cut into a wall that had been whitewashed with plaster and which, contrary to the other walls of the vault, was just a stone-wall partition that impeded access to the **Burial Chamber** once all the shrines and sarcophagi had been deposited inside. The floor in the **Burial Chamber**, like the one in the Annexe, was 3 feet 1 inch below the level of the **Antechamber**. The walls had an east-west orientation and were covered in plaster, although they had been painted yellow and decorated with ornaments that according to Carter were *"basic, classical and extremely austere."* Four niches had been carved into each of the walls of the room and each contained a magical figurine: *Anubis* on the western wall, *Osiris* on the eastern one, a djed pillar in the South and a shabti in the North. A hole had been pierced in the western wall: it was neither sealed nor blocked off and led the way into the fourth and last room. *"With a swift glance we realised this room held the most beautiful treasures in the tomb"*, says **Carter**, which is why he called it the **Treasury**. It had a north-south orientation and was unmarked and bore no decorations, like all the rooms except the **Burial Chamber.**

Pages 38-39
Reconstruction of Tutankhamun's tomb

Tutankhamun's tomb received number 62 in the official numeration archaeologists gave the tombs found in the Valley of the Kings at the beginning of the Twentieth Century. It is one of the smallest tombs of the royal necropolis, consisting of a stairway and a slightly sloped passageway leading to four rooms: the Antechamber, the Burial Chamber, the Treasury and the Annexe. This reconstruction shows the state it was in when Carter and his team found it.

Watercolour by J.-C. Golvin.

TUTANKHAMUN'S TOMB

ANNEXE
14 feet 27 inches long,
8 feet 5 inches wide,
8 feet 3 inches high.
Non-decorated walls.
Albeit small, this cramped room contained the greatest number of objects in the tomb: at least two thousand objects (half of what was found in the whole sepulchre). Sometimes the objects were found in piles as tall as 6 feet 5 inches high, which made it quite difficult for archaeologists to carry out their work. The collection of objets discovered in this room were of an extremely varied nature: shabtis, funerary furniture (beds, chairs, stool, tables…), glass cups, walking sticks, crooks, baskets, games, shields, weapons, breast-plates, wine decanters, pottery…

BURIAL CHAMBER
20 feet 9 inches long,
20 feet 9 inches long,
11 feet 9 inches high.
Walls decorated with funerary scenes.
The Burial Chamber contained objects that were designed to protect Tutankhamun's mummy: four shrines, found one inside the other, enclosed a stone sarcophagus, which contained the three coffins, the last of which was made of solid gold and held the royal mummified body. It was found dressed in its greatest ornaments: gold mask, circlet, jewellery, amulets…).

FORTH SEALED DOORWAY
Door that was blocked and covered with the impression of different seals

THIRD SEALED DOORWAY
Door that was blocked and covered with the impression of different seals.

TREASURY
15 feet 5 inches long,
12 feet 4 inches wide,
7 feet 6 inches high.
Non-decorated walls.
More than five hundred funerary objects were found in the Treasury: the shrine-shaped chest containing Canopic jars, funerary boats, statues of divinities, naos, small shrines, ritual objects, shabtis…

SECOND SEALED DOORWAY
Door that was blocked and covered with the impression of different seals

SLIGHT SLOPED PASSAGE
26 feet 5 inches long,
5 feet 5 inches wide,
6 feet 5 inches high.
Non-decorated walls.
When it was discovered, it was full of rubble, amongst which Howard Carter found a series of objects, some broken and some intact.

ANTECHAMBER
25 feet 7 inches long,
11 feet 6 inches wide,
8 feet 7 inches high.
Non-decorated walls.
Plunderers probably visited the Antechamber twice during ancient times. It still contained around seven hundred objects: dismantled chariots, funerary beds, chests, chairs, thrones, naos, boxes of food, protective statues…

FIRST SEALED DOORWAY
When it was discovered it was blocked by rubble, had a plaster coating and bore many seal impressions.

STAIRWAY
5 feet 5 inches wide.
Its sixteen steps led the way to the entrance of the tomb.

N

0   2,5   5 m

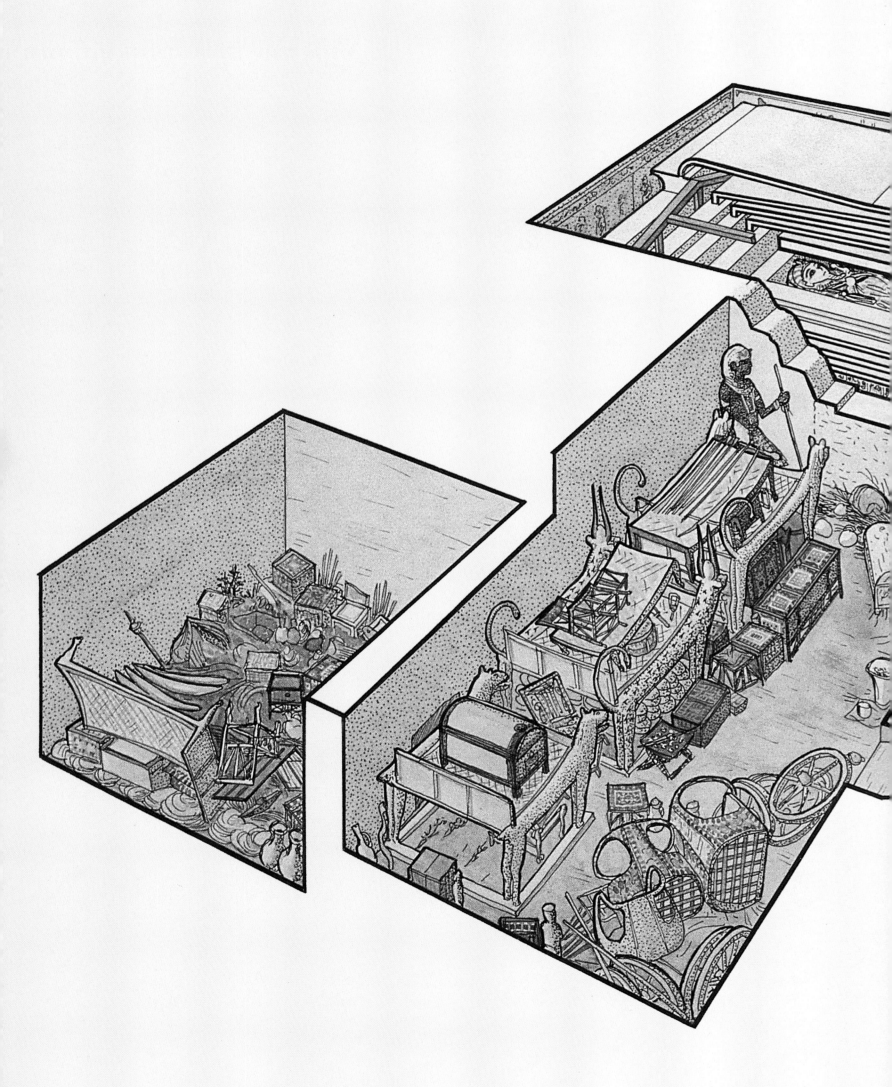

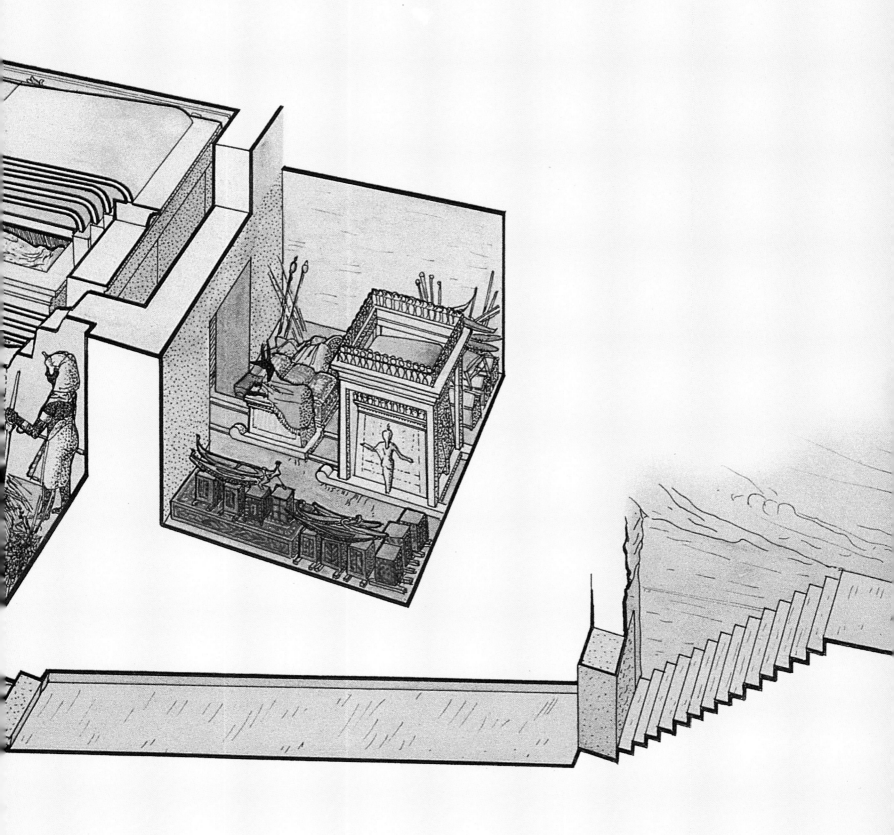

Ancient robberies in Tutankhamun's tomb

"A troubling fact that we had missed so far, suddenly hit us. Now that the whole door was visible, we could see it had already been reopened." On the 24th of November, the day when the stairway that led to the tomb was cleared, the team saw the whole door; that was the moment when **Carter** noticed a flaw. The door seemed to have been broken into, and it was now clear that it bore more than one type of seal: **Tutankhamun's** seal appeared on the part that remained untouched, and had not been opened since it was officially closed during the burial ritual. However, the seal of the necropolis was stamped on parts of the door where it had been replastered. Therefore, Carter came to the conclusion that the tomb had probably been entered twice after the king had been interred. There were many traces that showed that these robberies had taken place shortly after the funerary ceremony.

Carter managed to put together the story of the different robberies that took place in **Tutankhamun's** tomb through studying the findings he made during his work. When the sepulchre was discovered, the passage was totally packed with rubble and presented traces of having been entered. He noticed a tunnel had been dug out on the top left hand corner of the replastered door, and had then been resealed using small blocks of a slightly darker shade than the original ones. One would imagine that the first time the plunderers entered the tomb the passage was unobstructed, given the articles that were dug up under the rubble: pieces of pottery, fragments of various objects, lids of clay jars, vases, alabaster containers, strips of fabric… The objects that were revealed came from two places: some were remnants of the king's mummification process and the funerary banquet, most of which had been moved to well n°. 54 after the first robbery took place. The rest of the objects, mostly made of metal, had been discarded hastily by the plunderers. After this first incident, the necropolis officials most probably decided to reseal the tomb more efficiently: they filled the passage with rubble, hoping to block out any other intruders, and then affixed their seals. We do not know the extent of the theft or what rooms the plunderers entered on that occasion.

Not long after the first attempt was carried out a group of plunderers tried their luck with the pharaoh's tomb once again. The first thing they had to do was clear the inaccessible passageway, thus the plunderers decided to dig a tunnel on the left-hand side of the replastered area, just wide enough to allow a man to squeeze into it. The plunderers probably made a chain and passed each other the baskets there in the gloom, half-lit by the feeble light of an oil-lamp. *"It probably took them seven or eight hours to reach the second sealed doorway"*, remarked **Carter**, adding that *"It was then in the half-darkness that they started the robbery. They searched for gold, but they had to be able to carry the objects they found. It must have been pure torture to see all the gold glistening before them, all those objects they would not be able to remove due to their size or the amount of time it would take to move them."* The fact is, when they reached the **Antechamber** they were confronted by two new obstacles: lack of time and the evacuation of the loot. They must be quick, and due to the narrow tunnel they had to pick the most precious and less cumbersome items, since they could not remove any large objects.

In all likelihood, the plunderers managed to enter the whole tomb. They started with the **Antechamber** and the **Annexe**, emptying boxes, baskets and chests to inspect the objects they held. Then they broke away the seal on the doorway that led to the **Burial Chamber** and made their way to the **Treasury** where they simply opened a few jewellery boxes in great haste. However, one question still hangs in the air: how did the robbery end? It probably did not come to a natural end. Certain findings indicate the plunderers were caught red-handed. **Carter** noticed an interesting detail in the **Antechamber**: he found a bundle of solid gold rings wrapped in a piece of linen and hidden in a chest. The robbers would not have left behind an object that was so easy to carry if they had not been caught. However, it is difficult to know whether they were caught still inside the tomb or in their getaway.

When the officials of the royal necropolis discovered this second robbery, they decided to put an end to these intrusions and resealed the tomb. However, for unknown reasons, they acted as hastily as the bandits: they left the **Annexe** in the state they found it, collected the objects that had been strewn on the floor in the **Antechamber,** and placed them in chests and on funerary beds or stacked them up against the walls. After doing this they replastered and sealed some of the inner doorways, and filled the tunnel that had been dug out in the passage. Thus, they reclosed the entrance to the sepulchre and affixed their seal on the doorway.

Working methods

When **Carter** and his team entered the tomb on the 27th of November 1922 to carry out a more extensive analysis of its layout, they realised they would encounter many difficulties during the clearing processes. The state in which the plunderers had left the more than two thousand objects found in the **Annexe**, made **Carter** comprehend the problems this discovery would entail. *"We began to realise the actual size of the challenge we had before us, and saw that all the responsibilities would lie on our shoulders. We would not be able to make an inventory in just one season, this was not an ordinary find. We had no pattern to follow, this had never happened before... We thought the task was too much for any team to carry out, no matter how many men took part..."* Everything should be under control so that none of the marvellous objects and the information contained within, got lost in the process. The first thing to do was equip certain rooms to make them suitable for developing photographs and restoring objects. The vault belonging to *Sety II*, located at quite a distance in the south-western region, was used as a photography studio and restoration laboratory. Tomb nº. 55, located a few metres to the north of *Tutankhamun's* tomb, was used as a dark room. Then they tried to establish an effective system by which to enumerate the objects found in the tomb. They had to find a way to list objects that were stacked up, entangled or hidden in the chests, and which could not been seen at a glance. Initially, each batch was given a number: from 1 to 620 throughout the whole tomb. Each object that was taken from a certain batch was given a letter (from a to z) or a group of letters (from aa to zz, then aaa to zzz). When many objects were extracted from a certain batch, the lettering was shortened by using 4a instead of aaaa. For example, the ornaments found on the royal mummy correspond to batch number 256. It contained another one hundred and ten batches, numbered from 256a, which identified the gold mask, to 256-4v (or 256-vvvv), which corresponded to the last amulet. Some objects received the same numbers as others, and were catalogued using "b", which referred to objects that were identical or had the same nature: objects numbers 256-4i and 256-4i"b" are two amulets with the image of a vulture. All the objects found in the tomb were listed in this way, except for the last batch found in the **Annexe:** it held one hundred and twenty-three objects that were numbered from 620:1 to 620:123.

Once they had solved the problems relating to accommodating the rooms and the inventory, they established a method that could be carried out properly, systematically and effectively. At first, **Harry Burton**, the photographer that had been sent by the Department of Egyptian Antiquities of the **Metropolitan Museum of Art**, New York, took preliminary views of the rooms where work was being carried out. After attaching a small label that indicated their catalogue number, he took close-ups of groups of objects, sorting them from most to least important. By doing so, all the references appeared in at least one of the photos, thus one could also tell, by looking at each photograph, exactly where each batch had been found in the sepulchre. When the whole tomb had been photographed, the draughtsmen drew up a scale plan of the room that would reflect the numbers given to the objects in the inventory. This task was carried out initially by **Walter Hauser** and **Lindsley Foote,** both architects from the **Metropolitan Museum of Art**, New York. Unfortunately, they left the team after the Antechamber had been cleared, thus the crew had to proceed without them. So as to complete the information that appeared on photographs and sketches, the researchers wrote up an index card for each object where they stated the catalogue number, a brief description, the state it was found in and, if needed, complementary observations. **Arthur Callender** and **Carter** usually carried this out. It was now possible to start moving the objects. Sometimes, paraffin wax or a celluloid solution was applied to some objects since they were too fragile to be transported and crumbled when touched. When the object seemed sturdy enough, once it had undergone the first treatment, it was placed on a stretcher and taken to the laboratory that had been set up in the tomb of *Sety II*. Chemical engineer, **Alfred Lucas**, and assistant restoration professional to the **Metropolitan Museum of Art**, New York, **Arthur Mace**, carried out a strict restoration process. In most cases, they applied provisional preservative treatments, which were essential to allow for the transportation of the objects from **Luxor** to **Cairo**. If the object bore any inscriptions, **Alan Gardiner** was called in; he was a philologist who had been placed in charge of analysing the texts. After all this, the final index card could be written up. It contained all the information pertaining to the object's history: measurements, drawings found on the stairway and noted in situ, notes regarding inscriptions and a detailed description thereof, the type of preservative treatment applied, photographic dossier (with images of the object in its environment, in isolation, and when they depicted boxes full of many objects, shots of each stage of their extraction,…)

They still had to decide how the objects were going to be taken to **Cairo.** They had to pack all the material as carefully as possible, to protect the objects from dust and impacts. Each object was wrapped individually in a piece of cloth, then placed in a box, which was then stored in thick wooden crates. It took eighty-nine boxes to store all the objects found in the **Antechamber** (not counting the furniture that could not be stored this way). The boxes were filled with about 5000 feet of cotton and stored in another thirty-four crates. It was extremely hard to organise their transportation. They rapidly decided to transport the objects from **Thebes** to **Cairo** on the steamboat belonging to the Department of Antiquities. Given that the **Valley of the Kings** was approximately 6 miles from the Nile, where they would

take the boat, they still had to resolve how to get the crates from the vault of *Sety II* to the jetty, along a path that was dangerous, rocky and quite uneven. After long discussions, they chose to use the railway. Both the closed crates and the solidly packed cumbersome objects were placed on trolleys. As there was no actual railway, they had to construct one for the occasion, however, they did not have enough tracks to cover the whole distance, and opted for a difficult solution: they would lay down the tracks as they went along, lifting the tracks that had already been used and placing them back down again ahead of the trolleys, carrying the rails in a continuous chain. Around five hundred workmen and about fifteen hours of work were needed to perform this scheme. When they reached the Nile, the objects were loaded onto the steamboat and were to arrive in **Cairo** in a week. A few objects were transported differently: the gold mask and the king's inner sarcophagus travelled by train. The Department of Antiquities put a "special carriage" at **Carter's** disposition; it was to be watched over by armed guards. On arriving in **Cairo's** central station, the wagon was immediately taken to the **Egyptian Museum.**

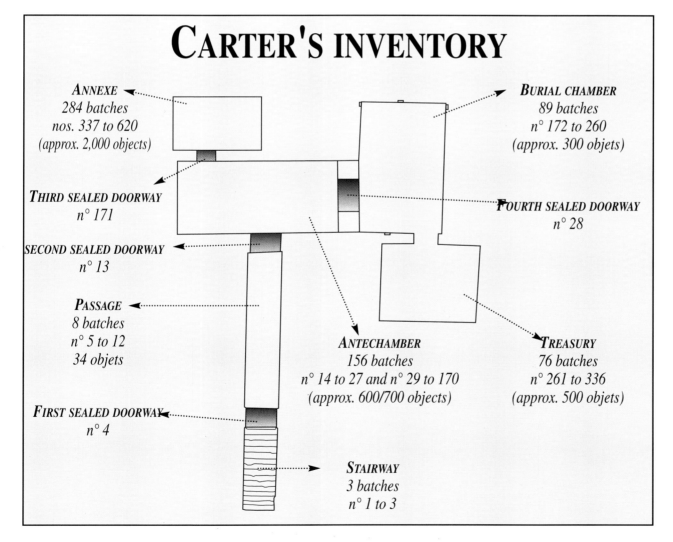

CARTER'S INVENTORY

ANNEXE
284 batches
nos. 337 to 620
(approx. 2,000 objects)

BURIAL CHAMBER
89 batches
n° 172 to 260
(approx. 300 objets)

THIRD SEALED DOORWAY
n° 171

FOURTH SEALED DOORWAY
n° 28

SECOND SEALED DOORWAY
n° 13

PASSAGE
8 batches
n° 5 to 12
34 objets

ANTECHAMBER
156 batches
n° 14 to 27 and n° 29 to 170
(approx. 600/700 objects)

TREASURY
76 batches
n° 261 to 336
(approx. 500 objets)

FIRST SEALED DOORWAY
n° 4

STAIRWAY
3 batches
n° 1 to 3

Batches and objects

This plan indicates the number of batches, the numbers given to the objects, and the total approximate number of objects that were found, in relation to the different architectural elements in Tutankhamun's tomb (passage, sealed doors and rooms). In total, Carter and his team numbered three thousand five hundred objects, in six hundred and twenty batches.

THE ANTECHAMBER
FIRST HOPES...

From autumn 1922 to winter 1923

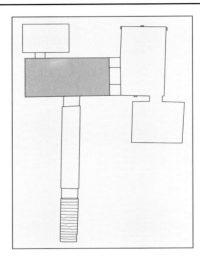

A formal ceremony was celebrated on the 29th of November 1922 to mark the official opening of the **Antechamber**, and the clearing processes was then set in motion. The room had a north-south orientation, and was 25 feet 7 inches long and 11 feet 6 inches wide. The walls had been whitened with plaster, and were neither inscribed nor decorated. The floor was full of objects, stacked and piled on top of each other, there was an uncountable number of dismantled chariots, funerary beds, chests and caskets, protective statues and statuettes, small shrines, naos, chairs and thrones, boxes of food... The **Antechamber** held one hundred and sixty-five batches containing approximately six or seven hundred objects in total, which were catalogued from nos. 14 to 27 and nos. 29 to 170. When the tomb was officially opened, **Carter** and **Carnarvon** had already conjured up a mental picture of what the **Antechamber** could hold. When the rubble had been cleared from the passage on the 26th of November, they had not been able to resist taking a peek at the secrets the tomb enclosed. They had pierced a small hole in the sealed doorway that separated the **Antechamber** from the passage, and saw «*wonderful things*», «*strange animals, statues and gold. Especially gold, everything shone with a golden lustre.*»

They widened the hole a little and entered the room to examine the treasures more closely. The tomb had been visited by plunderers who entered the **Antechamber** twice before it had been left to oblivion. In this case, unlike in the **Annexe**, the necropolis officials had made an attempt to slightly tidy the objects. They had collected them hastily and crammed them into boxes, without bothering to place them in their original containers: some chests were completely full, others were empty, the furniture had been stacked carelessly against the walls...

Thus, clearing the **Antechamber** was going to be a difficult task: they had to organise themselves to ensure the objects were listed, photographed, extracted and restored, all in the best conditions. The decision came quickly: the hypogeum of *Sety II* would be used as a restoration laboratory and storeroom, whereas tomb n°. 55 would become the photographic studio. The work began on the 27th of December: **Burton** took photographs, **Hall** and **Hauser** sketched, **Carter** and **Callender** wrote up the preliminary observations, cleared objects and moved them to the tomb of *Sety II*, where **Lucas** and **Mace** restored them. The clearing was carried out systematically: they started with the room's north-eastern wing, to the right of the doorway, and worked anticlockwise.

Chests, caskets and boxes

The tomb contained about fifty chests, in all shapes and sizes, and made in incredible materials and colours. There were many different types of chests, but the three most predominant were the coffer for cosmetic or small objects, the portable chest to store funerary material and the cabinet on high legs. Whatever their use, their shape was usually rectangular; however, this room contained four cartouche-shaped boxes and one semicircular one. Their lids were sometimes affixed and sometimes removable, and either flat, rounded or hinged. They were shut tightly by means of a rope that was wound around two knobs, one on one side of the chest and the other on the lid. After the rope had been wound round the lid, it was stamped with a seal before finally closing the box. However, when the tomb was discovered, all the chests had been emptied of their treasures, and did not contain the objects they originally enclosed. This has been deduced through the hieratic inscriptions found on the sides of certain chests that enumerated (sometimes in great detail), the objects originally contained within. For example, the two chests that were found in the entrance passage which were probably used by the plunderers to transport their loot bore the inscriptions of their contents. The first contained «*several shawls made of very good quality material, 2; 10 scarves, 20 long loincloths, 7 long shirts and 39 articles made of high-quality linen.*» The second contained «*a khenem vase and three silver milk jars.*»

These wooden chests made up most of the collection, be they painted, plated, gold coated or inlaid. Nonetheless, **Carter's** team also found ten boxes made of calcite, ivory, gold reeds or papyrus fibres. Whatever the material used, the crafting of these chests was quite mediocre: they were not at all crafted in a professional manner, the painting was quite average and the finishing touches had been made hastily.

Chest (n°. 44)

This chest is unique because the form of the sloping lid is that of Per-wer, the ancient Southern shrine. The sculptors alternated royal cartouches and uraei on the long sides, and the small sides were decorated with two representations of Heh, god of Eternity, that surround the sovereign's name and prenomen. The chest was closed with a rope that had been wound around the two faience knobs, one on the lid and the other on the chest itself, and then sealed.

Golden plated wood with faience inlays.
Tomb n°. 62, Antechamber.
The Cairo Museum.

One of the most impressive caskets found in the tomb was stored near the threshold of the **Antechamber**, next to an alabaster vase and two funerary bouquets. **Carter** described it as *«one of the most beautiful artistic treasures found in the tomb, no photograph or description could ever render its delicate paintings, which far surpass anything ever found here in Egypt.»*

It is carved in stucco wood and then painted, 24 inches long and 17 inches high. The main sides are decorated with pictures representing war scenes in which **Tutankhamun** is ever-present: on one side he fights the Africans and on the other he confronts the Asians. Both sides of the casket represent the same images: the triumphant Pharaoh holds the reins of the chariot, piercing enemies' bodies with his arrows. His fan-bearers and his chariot guard appear behind him on three levels, whilst in front of him, his adversaries lie defeated: dogs attack wounded warriors and the survivors are taken prisoner. The sun disc and the royal vultures appear above **Tutankhamun's** carriage, giving him protection.

The sides of the casket are perfectly symmetrical: two cartouches bearing the king's name and prenomen appear in the centre of the composition; on either side, the king is depicted as a sphinx trampling upon his enemies. The rounded lid is decorated with hunting scenes: on the first side the king is striking down lions;

on the second, antelopes, hyenas, ostriches and desert animals. These delicate and precise representations are painted in tempera on a stucco wood base. When the **Antechamber** was being cleared, the casket was immediately taken to the restoration laboratory to repair any fragile elements and restore the paintings. Two preservative treatments were applied to stabilise the object: a celluloid solution and paraffin wax. All there was left to do was open the casket and see what treasures it contained; **Carter** recounts: *«We had an idea of how difficult a task this would be, we knew it would take us about three weeks to get to the bottom of the casket. On the right-hand side, at the top, sat a pair of rush and papyrus sandals which were in perfect condition; under them was a gilt headrest, and beneath that, a mass of bundled clothes, of gold and of leather, which we could make nothing of. On the left, a superb royal robe covered in beadwork, and, in the top corner, beads carved rudimentarily out of black resin.»*

This jumble had probably been caused by the necropolis officials when they hastily «tidied» the sepulchre after the second robbery took place and it caused **Carter** some serious restoration problems. In his opinion it would have been better to leave the objects on the floor or wherever the plunderers had thrown them, instead of cramming them savagely into the boxes.

Chest (n°. 21)

The delicate decorations and harmonious colouring on this chest have made it one of the master-pieces of Tutankhamun's tomb. The scenes that are represented on the long sides and the lid depict the king in his chariot, beating down his enemies or hunting desert animals. The smaller sides bear two sphinxes with human heads that support the royal cartouches.

Painted stucco wood.
Tomb n°. 62, Antechamber.
The Cairo Museum.

Portable chest (n°. 32)

Elegant but sober, this casket is one of the few portable chests that have been found intact upon discovery in Egypt. Once it has been set in place, the sliding poles can be pushed back into the body of the casket, which can then be used as a simple indoor chest.

Ebony and cedar-wood casket inlaid with ivory.
Tomb n°. 62, Antechamber.
The Cairo Museum.

According to **him**, the worst thing was *«to have packed them together with the oddest objects.»* The portable chest (n°. 32) was found on the lion-headed funerary bed, and is also considered one of the most beautiful chests found in the tomb. The main structure is made of ebony, enclosing lighter cedar-wood panels that are highlighted with a double band of ivory. The cornice, in the shape of a «cavetto corniche», rests on a golden rim, and its legs are square and compact, with bronze glides. The lid is triangular, and made of the same material as the whole casket: ebony frame, double band of ivory and cedar-wood panels. It must have been extremely heavy when full, being 32 inches long and 25 inches high; thus sliding poles had been attached to carry it by. The four independent wooden poles were found in a completely preserved state, the visible part was rounded and the other had a stopper on the end. When the casket was not going to be moved anymore, the poles could be pushed back into the body of the structure, which then became a simple chest that could be used indoors. The chest was decorated in great sobriety: simply surrounded by strips of hieroglyphic texts inscribed on the ebony jambs and a single historical

event that is engraved on the light wood panel that bears the closure knob. In this representation, *Tutankhamun* is depicted wearing the war crown, and presenting an offering of burning resin and wine to a divinity named *«Unennefer, at the head of the Occident, Great Lord and Master of the Necropolis»*, i.e. *Osiris*, the lord of the deceased. The inscriptions are finely crafted hieroglyphs inlaid in white paste.

All the formulae are constructed similarly, and all start with the same structure: *«Words spoken by,»* followed by the name of one of the great divinities of the pantheon *(Thoth, Geb, Ra-Harakhty, Ptah-Sokar-Osiris,...)* who then speaks to the pharaoh ensuring him protection, resurrection, rebirth and bliss. In compensation, the king offers them an infinite amount of gifts; all the structures that refer to these acts begin with *«Offers made by the king.»* There are also four columns that have been reserved to enumerating the titles the king and his wife possess: *«King of Upper and Lower Egypt, the Master of the Two Lands, Nebkheperura, Son of Ra, beloved, Tutankhamun, Ruler of Upper Egyptian Heliopolis»*, and for the queen *«Great Royal Wife, beloved, Lady of the Two Lands, Ankhesenamun.»*

Ceremonial carriages and functional chariots

"Parts of chariots were piled up in disarray all along the south wall and as far as the entrance doorway. Evidently, they had been heaped together by the plunderers, who had turned them upside down to grasp the gold decorations that covered them; however, this was not the only reason they were in this state. The entrance passage was terribly narrow; therefore, to allow for the chariots to be introduced into the chamber, the axles have been sawn in two deliberately and the wheels dismantled. It will obviously take us a great amount of time to re-assemble the chariots, but the results will be well worth our troubles. They are totally gilt, their surface is decorated either with scenes sculpted on the gold itself or inlaid designs of coloured glass paste or small stones." The clutter the south-east corner of the room was in caught Carter's attention from the moment he set foot in the Antechamber, a jumble of gold-plated wooden articles was lying there, all of which were probably parts of these chariots."

Tutankhamun's tomb held six chariots in all: four were found in the **Antechamber** and two in the **Treasury**. They must have been dismantled, the axles sawn in half, before being placed in the tomb for two reasons: the first was the narrowness of the actual passage, the second was the amount of space they would take up once inside the tomb; hence the dismantling, which would reduce the cluttering of the tomb. It must have been extremely difficult for the Egyptologists who were in charge of these objects as all the pieces had to be taken apart before they could be mounted once again to become a coherent structure. The first step was to loosen the wooden parts that were trapped and tangled together under the harnesses or other leather parts. «Exposure to humidity», says **Carter**, «*turns undressed leather into an ugly blackish glue. Luckily, these leather parts are usually plated with gold and, thus, well preserved. Therefore, we hope their reconstruction will be carried out without too much effort.*» In fact, five of the six chariots were totally reconstructed (the four found in the **Antechamber** and one from the **Treasury**).

The two most beautiful carriages found in the vault were the king's ceremonial carriages, nos. 120 and 122 which were most probably used for official ceremonies and parades. The body is of gilt stucco wood, rectangular in shape, measuring more in width than in depth; it is open-backed and both its inner and outersides are completely decorated. A guardrail, which leans on the yoke, has been mounted on the front part of the body, to increase the stability of the passenger during the ride. The lower part of the yoke is slightly curved, and is made of a single piece of wood with long straight fibres that has been mounted onto the back crosspiece by means of a notch and secured to the front rail with two straps. A double beam, made of calcite and gilt wood, is secured to the end of the yoke by straps and dowels. The wheels are made of wood and then bound in leather, each has six spokes that join in the axle. However, when the carriages were found, only the body was attached to the axle, all the wheels had been sawn off. The bodies are noteworthy because of their carved decorations, enhanced by a strip inlaid with coloured glass paste and semi-precious stones. The first carriage, n°. 120, is particularly remarkable: the **Sema-tawi** is depicted in the centre of its inner side; symbolised by two emblematic plants, the papyrus representing Lower Egypt and the lotus representing Upper Egypt, which are linked around the the tracheas of two prisoners. This Egyptian manifestation depicts the *«Unification of the Two Lands»*, representing the union of the North and the South under one sovereign. This representation appears on a frieze that shows the captives, drawn in an extremely realistic fashion, tied by ropes that end at times in a papyrus flower and others in a lotus bud, meant to signify that they now belong either to Northern or to Southern countries. On either side, the king appears in sphinx form, protected by a vulture; in one instance he tramples an African, in another he faces an Asian; a decorative rosette appears between them which, given the decoration of the whole piece, seems to have been placed there at a later time.The two other chariots found in the **Antechamber** are of much lighter consistency, specially the undecorated open-sided vehicle with solid wood wheels (n°. 161). In **Carter's** opinion it was probably a functional carriage. Only one of the two chariots found in the **Treasury** could be reconstructed (n°. 333). These were also hunting vehicles, although they were not open and had not been hollowed out, as **Carter** discovered the remains of the leather side-walls. One bore no special decoration, the other was highly decorated and coloured.

Thrones, stools and couches

There were three different types of chairs found in the **Antechamber** and the **Annexe** of *Tutankhamun's* tomb: six royal couches, a low-backed piece and twelve stools. There were also eleven rectangular foot stools, which could be placed in front of the chair, some rush-work cushions and a wooden folding canopy. The most impressive piece of the group, one of the «*tomb's greatest treasures*», was found in the **Antechamber**, stored under the funerary bed decorated with the hippopotamus head. «*The throne* (n^c. 91), *was completely coated with gold, richly adorned with glass, faience and precious stones. Its legs had been fashioned in feline form, and were surmounted by lion's heads, fascinating in their power and simplicity. Superb crowned and winged serpents formed the arms of the throne. Between the bars that supported the back appeared six protective cobras, carved in the wood, gilt and inlaid. However, the back panel was the most glorious element of the throne, I immediately claimed it was the most beautiful thing I had seen in Egypt.*»

The scene depicts *Ankhesenamun* perfuming her husband's chest whilst he is seated on his throne. She is wearing a long linen robe and a high composite crown, in one hand she holds a small jar of ointment and with the other she gently adds some touches of perfume to the king's collar. *Tutankhamun* sits comfortably on his throne, surrounded by cushions in a casual attitude, one arm resting on his knee, the other thrown over the back of the throne.

The royal couple are in one of the halls of the palace, lined with flowered columns, a frieze of cobras above them and a base with steps below them. *Aten*, the sun disc, appears at the top of the composition, shooting down his rays with his hands outstretched towards the young couple. Although the colours are now slightly faded, they are still bright and harmonious: crowns, decorations, collars and jewellery are all inlaid with glazed clay, coloured glass paste or precious stones. The clothing is silver-coated and the back is covered in sheets of gold. Despite the impressive beauty of the object, this is not its only noticeable aspect, the iconography represented is also noteworthy. The scene gives evidence of the religious events that were taking place during that period in time, after the Amarnian period when *Akhenaten* imposed *Aten* as the divine god, until the worshipping of *Amun* was reinstated during the first years of *Tutankhamun's* reign. The scene that is depicted on the back panel of the throne is still inspired by that Amarnian period: the sun disc surrounded by cartouches that still name *Aten* as the main god, the stylistic and artistic forms and the simple scene depicted in the representation, part of the couple's everyday life. However, it is still ambiguous due to the fact that the names of the couple are mixed: in some cartouches they appear as *Tutankhaten* and *Ankhesenpaaten*, whilst in others (where there are signs of *Aten's* name being hammered out), they have become Tutankhamun and *Ankhesenamun*. The chair was probably constructed whilst *Akhenaten* was still alive and the family still living in **Tell el-Amarna**. After the schism that restored faith in *Amun* took place, the workers tried to adapt it to the new religious beliefs, to make it worthy of the pharaoh's tomb, although they did not manage to finish this renovation.

A wooden chair (n°. 87) was also found in the **Antechamber** and is one of the most elegant seats found in the sepulchre. It is carved in thick red-coloured wood which could be cedar-wood, rosewood, a type of fir tree or even a strange Egyptian species. Whatever the nature of the wood, its dark colour contrasts greatly with the light sheets of gold that decorate some parts of the chair. The curved nature of the stool indicates it was meant to hold a cushion. It is held together with a mortice and tenon joint that is strengthened by bronze rivets with golden tips. The legs end in lion paws, and the back is decorated with an open-work representation of **Heh**, god of Eternity. The papyrus and ebony couch is quite similar to the aforementioned chair, although it has not been preserved as well due to the fragile material it is constructed from. It was also found in the **Antechamber** on top of a pile of objects found on the cow-headed funerary bed and was given number 82.

The last chair in the **Antechamber** is known as the chair made for *Tutankhamun* as a child (n°. 39). It was found on the lion-headed funerary bed, and is similar in shape to the gilt throne, but quite a lot smaller, being 28 inches high. It was probably created for a child aged between seven or nine years old, and could have

Chair with the image of Heh (n°. 87)

The back panel is adorned with an image of Heh, god of Eternity. Kneeling on the nub sign, symbol of gold, he holds palm-tree leaves; from his right arm hangs an ankh cross, symbol of life. All these symbols appear to ensure the king has a long and prosperous life in the Netherworld. On either side of the divinity, Tutankhamun with the «Horus» name appears, «Powerful bull, satisfied since his birth», his head is surrounded by the «He of the sedge and bee» name, «Ra's supreme manifestation», and the «Son of Ra» name, «Living image of Amun, Lord of Southern Heliopolis.» A long sheet of gold has been placed on the top of the back, it represents the sun disc, flanked by two uraei, the cobra that could crush Ra's enemies and, thus, the king's too.

Wood with ivory.
Tomb n°. 62, Antechamber.
The Cairo Museum.

Gold-plated throne (n°. 91)

Carter described it as "one of the greatest treasures" of the whole tomb. It differs from others in its technique and decoration which is heavily influenced by Amarnian canons. Aten crowns the composition with his sun disc, who was named the dynastic divinity by the heretic pharaoh Amenhotep IV-Akhenaten.

Gold-coated wood inlaid with glass paste, faience and semi-precious stones.
Tomb n°. 62, Antechamber.
The Cairo Museum.

Chair made for Tutankhamun as a child (n°. 39)

Classical in its construction, with a slightly inclined back, curved seat and legs ending in lion paws risen on bronze drums. It is held together by means of a mortice and tenon joint, strengthened with small bronze dowels, with gilt heads. It consists of four wooden rungs, ending in ivory floral motifs. The back panel is inlaid with ivory on an ebony backdrop. It has simple geometric decorations, the two armrests are decorated both on the inner and outer side with fine gilt panels: some represent entwined branches, others recumbent animals.

Ebony with gold and ivory incrustations.
Tomb n°. 62, Antechamber.
The Cairo Museum.

belonged to *Tutankhamun* before he was crowned king of Egypt. It is totally unmarked, made of African ebony and inlaid with gold and ivory.

This chair (n°. 351) was found in the south-east angle of the **Annexe** draped in sheets of linen and is known as the «Episcopal throne» or «ecclesiastical throne» given its similarity to the faldstool used by the Christian bishops. It is one of the finest sculpted masterpieces of the tomb, with a slightly inclined back and curved seat which is fixed to a folding stool. Carved in ebony, gold-plated in some places and inlaid with small stones, coloured glass paste, pieces of multicoloured faience and ivory. The actual seat is decorated to imitate leopard-skin. It rests upon folding legs that end in duck heads, linked together by a fine decoration of papyrus and lotus stems that represent the **Sema-tawi**, unification of Upper and Lower Egypt. The back panel presents a geometric ornamentation that is placed around three pillars of text that refer to the king's titularity, alongside the names of *Amun* and *Aten*. *Nekhbet*, the protector of Egypt, appears overhead, depicted as a vulture with outstretched wings, holding an ostrich feather in her talon, symbol of *Maat*, goddess of truth and justice. A series of royal cartouches have been imprinted on either side. The composition is dominated by the sun disc of *Aten*, surrounded by a frieze of **uraei**. The most interesting feature of this chair is the inscription of the names *Tutankhaten* and *Tutankhamun*, which demonstrates the religious upheaval that was taking place during the end of the 18th Dynasty.

N°. 349 is the least interesting royal chair. It was found near the **Annexe's** southern wing, piled with objects placed one on top of another. It resembles numbers 87 and 82, although it has much smaller dimensions, just 28 inches. It has a straight, high back, raised legs ending in lion paws, open-work **Sema-tawi** decoration between the legs, and no arm rests.

Among the other examples of this type of furniture, there are only a few noteworthy pieces. Twelve stools were discovered, their size, shape and finish are astounding, and no similar objects have been found in the tomb. The most beautiful, although not the richest, is the folding stool (n°. 83) found in the **Antechamber**, placed in front of the image of the hippopotamus goddess *Taweret*. These stools, simple in construction, are usually carved in wood, with folding legs, joined

two-by-two with a round bar, and topped by a seat that is often slightly curved so as to hold a cushion. *Tutankhamun's* folding stool was constructed following these patterns, and is remarkable because of the beauty of its decorations. The legs finish elegantly in duck heads, which are painted black and white, with a open beak that clasps the round bar. The seat is decorated with gilt designs that imitate leopard-skin. The stools which in long-gone eras were decorated with real animal skin most probably inspire this decoration. One detail confirms this theory: on one of the sides, the artist has placed a feline tail, with a gilt tip.

The other «gold **Sema-tawi**» stool (n°. 467) found nearly intact despite its location in the north-east angle of the **Annexe**, is also noteworthy. It was found upside down and trapped between the wall and a big wooden bed, on which it partially rested. It has straight legs and a curved seat, kept together by a mortice and tenon joint, strengthened by nails and bolts that are gilt and set in a decorative manner. A gold plated **Sema-tawi** emblem appears between the legs, which are slightly raised and sculpted with lion paws with golden claws.

Thrones and chairs usually have foot stools made to accompany them. These are small rectangular pieces, made to rest one's feet on when sitting down. **Tutankhamun's** tomb contained eleven in total: three of which were made for chairs 91, 87 and 351; the other eight are independent and less finely crafted. Apart from their functional use, they also had a strong symbolic connotation. On the top side two figures appear with their arms twisted behind their backs, they represent the *«leaders of all foreign countries, that are at the kings feet»*, one Sudanese and one Nubian represented the Southern countries (African race), a Syrian and a Libyan represented the Northern countries (Asian and Indo-European races); each can be recognised through itsiconography. When he was seated, the king could symbolically tread on his enemies.

The last noteworthy object is the wooden folding canopy (n°. 123). **Carter** believed *«it must have been part of the royal luggage and could be unwound manually to shield the king from the sun.»* A type of parasol even... The frame is composed of four vertical poles and twenty-eight horizontal boughs, over which a piece of linen was draped. Unfortunately, the canopy could not be totally rebuilt, as some of its elements could not be found.

53

The ritual couch with hippopotamus (n°. 137)

Three identical couches were found along the western wall of the Antechamber: they had been designed to help the king on his celestial journey. The hippopotamus has a fierce appearance and could possibly represent goddess Taweret or the «Devourer of the dead».

Gilt wood inlaid with glass paste and elements made of ivory.
Tomb n°. 62, Antechamber.
The Cairo Museum.

Funerary beds and functional beds

Carter explains how, on first inspection, he was surprised at the finding of the three big funerary beds lined up against the western wall of the **Antechamber** of the tomb. He remembers seeing silhouettes that *«resembled monstrous animals,»* which projected their terrifying shadow onto the walls. This type of furniture was not all together unknown to archaeologists, as they had appeared more than once on mural paintings found on the walls of tombs in the Theban necropolis.

However, a real example had never been discovered. The beds from *Tutankhamun's* tomb are made of wood and then gold-plated, the three are identical in their conception and are composed of many elements that can easily be dismantled: two poles made up the long stylish body and end in an animal head, a mattress that imitates the texture of a cushion, footboard, and a rectangular base onto which the animal legs were socketed. It was held together with hooks, rings and bronze brackets.

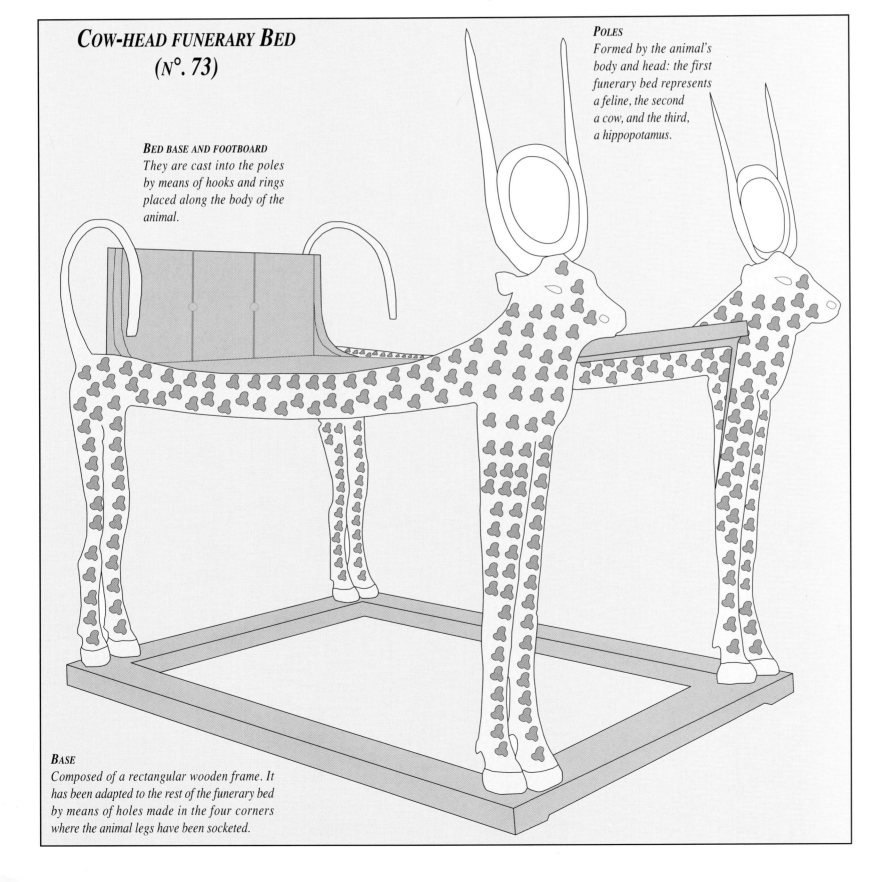

COW-HEAD FUNERARY BED (N°. 73)

BED BASE AND FOOTBOARD
They are cast into the poles by means of hooks and rings placed along the body of the animal.

POLES
Formed by the animal's body and head: the first funerary bed represents a feline, the second a cow, and the third, a hippopotamus.

BASE
Composed of a rectangular wooden frame. It has been adapted to the rest of the funerary bed by means of holes made in the four corners where the animal legs have been socketed.

Due to their height it is impossible to think these funerary beds were used when the king was living: they measure between 4 feet 4 inches and 5 feet high. Most probably they were simply funerary furniture used for rituals, entailing a strong magical-religious signification given by the animals sculpted on the poles. The first couch (n°. 35) represents a feline (lion or lioness) with extremely expressive features: crystal eyes which show the pupil and the iris that are painted black and two turquoise glass paste tears run down the cheeks and muzzle, the other details are simply carved into the gilt wood. On the front of the couch, on the board of the mattress and the bed-base, the «**He of the sedge and bee**» name appears alongside the name of the *Mehet-Weret* cow, the «Great Flood», a goddess who symbolises the primordial ocean that gave birth to the sun and the universe.

The second couch represents a cow with trefoiled patches made of dark blue glass paste inlaid in the body. On the heads the eyes are elegantly decorated and two long lyre-shaped horns that protrude and encompass the sun disc. The cow evidently represents the creative entity *Mehet-Weret*, whose «First Manifestation» was in the form of a cow floating over the *Nun*. The inscriptions engraved on the bed base confirm the identity of this animal: «*The god incarnate, who will live forever, the Lord of Two Lands who effects the kingship of Ra, Osiris, the king of the South, Nebkheperura* (**Tutankhamun's** prenomen), *the beloved of the goddess Isis-Mehet.*» The goddess' name has been engraved using a hieroglyphic sign that represents a cow-headed female divinity, bearing horns and the sun disc. In fact, as from the end of the 18th Dynasty, the names of the goddesses *Hathor, Isis* and *Mehet-Weret* (sometimes inscribed, as in this case, with a mix or association of her name) were used equally to refer to the heavenly cow.

The third couch (n°.137) was constructed to represent «The Devourer of the dead», a goddess with a hybrid physique consisting of the body and legs of a feline, a crocodile tail and a hippopotamus head. This animal appears to be especially ferocious given its open mouth, that reveals an ivory tongue (which has been tinted red) and ivory teeth. In the funerary context, this divinity usually appears in scenes that represent the final judgement and the weighing of the soul. If the judgement is unfavourable she then devours the soul of the deceased. This immense hippopotamus is also the

representation of *Taweret*, «The Great of death», sometimes depicted with a crocodile on her back, the goddess who brings children into the world and protects the new-borns.

Although these beds are used at vehicles that take the king on his journey to the heavens, it is difficult to know the precise role each bed plays in this ritual. At the most, an inscription found on the gold-plated shrine from the outermost part of the **Burial Chamber** reads that the cow-headed couch (and probably the lion-headed one also) was directly linked to the sun myth that appears in the «**Book of the Heavenly Cow.**» This story dates from the times when men and gods lived together on earth and recounts the last years of *Ra's* earthly reign and his rise towards the heavens. The story pertaining to the end of his reign tells of how, after fighting many enemies, *Ra* felt weary, tired and betrayed. Disappointed by the

Bed decorated with images of Bes (n°. 47)

Bes was a deformed gnome with jovial features and was one of the most important domestic protective divinities. At night he watches over the sleeping person, keeping hostile spirits and evil forces at bay. For this reason he appears regularly on footboards, as in the model created for young Tutankhamun.

Ebony, partially-gilt.
Tomb, n°. 62 Antechamber.
The Cairo Museum.

activities carried out by his own people and mankind, he summoned an assembly of the gods and explained his feelings. They advised him to recline on the goddess *Nut*'s back (who had transformed into a cow for the occasion). At dawn, the sun god saw his kingdom and noticed that the men bore bows and arrows and sticks, ready to fight among each other and said: «*Evil is behind you, slaughterers...*» Then, he begged *Nut* to take him away from this heartless land: «*Take me far away from them, lift me,*» he begged. Which is how the cow rode *Ra* to the heavens.

Apart from these three funerary beds another six beds were also found in the tomb: two in the **Antechamber** and four in the **Annexe**. These are purely functional objects, and all follow the same pattern: lion paw legs that rest on bronze drums; no bed head, rectangular ornamented footboards, mattress made up by a netting of entangled fabrics. The most beautiful piece is definitely the bed decorated with images of Bes (n°. 47) When the **Antechamber** was opened it was found on the lion-headed funerary bed, most probably placed there in ancient times by the high officials of the necropolis in their haste to tidy the room. On the mattress and all over the bed were a jumble of walking sticks, bows and arrows that had been emptied out of a nearby rectangular casket. The bed is carved in ebony and is partly gold-plated, its most distinguishable feature is the footboard, which is divided into three open-work panels that are decorated with the same composition. The figure of *Bes* is represented in the middle, facing forwards, and on either side of him, two lions appear portrayed sideways leaning on a sa (hieroglyphic symbol of protection). All three characters are wearing a crown symbolising an open lotus flower. The royal loin cloth, the mane and the crowns are carved in gold. *Bes* belongs to a category of gods that could give aid in adversity and were, therefore, popular in Egyptian households. His physiognomy emanates cheerfulness, happiness and joviality: he is a bearded deformed gnome, with twisted legs and joyful features. His main role was to protect mankind from evil beings or hostile spirits, and against harmful genii and reptiles, scorpions or any other dangerous beast. With his strange dances and funny faces he fights off evil spirits and impedes curses. He normally protects the household and watches over pregnant women and new-borns. It was believed that when everything is calm at night, he looked over those who slept, keeping the evil forces at bay. Thus his presence is essential and it is extremely advisable to keep an amulet bearing his image. In houses, small *Bes* figurines are left on small altars and windows, and in cases like **Tutankhamun's** tomb, footboards are decorated with his image.

Only two of the other five beds are noteworthy. The first one (n°. 466) was found upturned in the north part of the **Annexe**. It is smaller in size although its frame is quite elegant, made of ebony, covered by a thick sheet of gold. The footboard is decorated with three exquisitely sculpted panels, although they are not decorated with open-work decorations: in the centre appears the **Sema-tawi**, symbolising the Unification of Upper and Lower Egypt, and on either side bouquets of lotus flowers and various floral motifs. Given the scratches on the frame and the wear of the netting of the mattress, **Carter** thought this bed had been used before it was placed inside the royal tomb. However, given the state some of the objects found in the **Annexe** were in after the two robberies and the «tidying» carried out by the officials of the necropolis, this hypothesis can not be verified.

The second bed (n°. 586) was also found in the **Annexe**. It is a simple, folding bed, that is interesting because it is the only absolutely intact example made in pharaonic Egypt that has been found to date. Strangely enough, its structure resembles modern day design. It is only 12 inches high, has hinges on two points of its base that allow for the folding, when both extremities are closed together, it is barely 23 inches long. Like any other bed, it is held up by four legs: two at the front and two at the back which are all affixed to the main structure. The legs can also be folded at the hinges, thus reducing the size of the piece.

Shabtis

These figurines have been used since the Middle Kingdom. They were called **chaouabtis** (word derived from *chaouab* meaning «wood», the material they are carved from), and act as a «substitute» of the deceased; during that period, a deceased person only possessed one **chaouabti** which was placed next to him or her inside the sepulchre. With the wake of the New Kingdom, both the word and its function evolved: **chaouabtis** became **shabtis** (this time derived from the word *ousheb* meaning «answer»), and instead of substitutes, they became slaves and were packed, sometimes by hundreds, into the sepulchres. Their mission was to «answer» for the deceased when he or she was called to carry out farming chores or small material tasks executed in the Netherworld. This new mission is confirmed by the tools the figurines hold: yokes, baskets, picks and hoes and the small text that was usually carved or painted along their bodies (an excerpt from chapter VI of the «**Book of the Dead**»):«*Oh shabti, listen to me. I have been called to render the various tasks the deceased spirits must carry out in the Netherworld, you must know shabti, that you with your tools must obey the man and fulfil his needs. It will be you, shabti, who will be punished instead of me by the guards of the Dwat (the world of the dead): you will sow the fields, fill the canals with water and move the sand from east to west. Your answer will always be: I am here, awaiting orders.*»

Carter found four hundred and thirteen **shabtis** in *Tutankhamun's* tomb: three hundred and sixty-five were «workers», one for each day of the year; thirty-six were «guards» one for each decade (the decade was then a period of ten days); and twelve «guards», one for each month. They were found in twenty-four boxes in the **Annexe**, fourteen containing two hundred and thirty-six statuettes, and another ten boxes were found in the **Treasury** (containing one hundred and seventy-six statuettes). Only one **shabti** was found in the **Antechamber,** and is considered the most beautiful statue. n°. 110 was probably not placed there originally, according to **Carter** it was probably taken out of one of the boxes from the **Annexe.** The boxes are extremely rudimentarily carved; they are made of wood, twenty-three of them have been blackened with resin, and they are all on sleds; only one of them has been whitened with chalk. All of them are rectangular and have domed lids. The structure is closed by means of two knobs: one on one of the sides, the other on the lid, that are tied together with a small rope stamped with the seal of the necropolis: the jackal *Anubis* with nine captives.

The main trait of these figurines is the great diversity of their forms: the material used, the size, craftsmanship, complements and head-dress. Regarding the materials used to manufacture ***Tutankhamun's*** shabtis: some are wooden (carved, sculpted, painted or gilt), some are made of stone (limestone, granite, quartzite or calcite) and others are made of faience (blue, turquoise, violet or white). The tallest reach 26 inches high, an extremely tall measurement for this type of statuettes. Although some are crudely fashioned, others are considered masterpieces of Egyptian art. All **shabtis** wear a head-cloth: either a **khepresh** (a blue war crown, similar to a helmet, domed with round discs), the red crown of Upper Egypt or the **pschent** (a crown that mixes elements from the aforementioned crowns). Those that do not wear a head-cloth wear a short wig (known as the Nubian wig), a long wig with three layers or a **nemes** (striped headcloth that covers their shoulders). The foreheads of the **shabtis** are usually decorated with the cobra and the vulture that symbolise the goddesses *Wadjit* and *Nekhbet,* who protect Upper and Lower Egypt. Although this is not always the case, sometimes just the **uraeus** (the cobra that personifies the Sun eye) appears, none of the royal emblems are carved onto the figure. The complements they hold are diverse: all types of tools such as the **Nekhakha** flail and the heka sceptre, both royal insignias; two flails, two **ankh** crosses (symbol of life), the **ankh** cross and the flail, the **djed** pillar (symbol of strength and stability) and the flail; farming tools (hoes and baskets)... More than a third of the **shabtis** were empty-handed. Their bodies are covered in a mummiform shroud, although their arms are not enclosed, and are usually inscribed with either a long or short extract from chapter VI of the «**Book of the Dead**», or the names and titles of the sovereign. Carter found one thousand eight hundred and sixty-six tools, individually carved miniatures, that were complements for these statues: yokes, hoes, picks, ploughing tools and baskets, all made of iron or golden metal. There are six noteworthy **shabtis**: all of which bear an inscription on their feet that indicate they were an offering made for the king's funeral by the Royal scribe.

Tutankhamun's ka statues

On the 26th of November 1922, three days before officially opening the **Antechamber**, **Carter** and his team had already contemplated many of the objects hidden in the chamber through a small hole they pierced in the second sealed doorway. The two statues placed on either side of the blocked door that led to the **Burial Chamber** had captured their attention greatly. They «*looked like sentinels*» said **Carter** in his first report. Later on, once the chamber had been cleared, he added that «*the statues seemed strange and imposing when we first set eyes on them, surrounded by and partially hidden under many other objects. Now standing alone in the empty Antechamber, they are even more imposing.*» One can imagine the effect these two great statues caused on the archaeologists, looking at them through a hole and lit by just a dim torch. The fact that their shoulders were covered with shrouds –albeit partially decomposed when found– must have accentuated the striking effect of the vision.

Both similar in craftsmanship, they depict **Tutankhamun** standing upright, as if walking, the left foot slightly in front of the right one. They are 5 feet 7 inches tall –which according to the studies carried out by doctor **Douglas E. Derry**, who studied the mummy in November 1925, was about the real height of the pharaoh– and stand on a rectangular base that barely measures 8 inches. They are made of dark red wood and composed of different parts that have been put together by means of a series of hooks, they were also plastered to cover any irregularities or joints. The whole statue has been given a black resin coating, to imitate the king's skin, and other details such as wig, jewellery, loincloth, sandals and baton are gold-plated. His eyes are inlaid with fragments of hard obsidian and limestone, set in bronze, and his forehead bears a superbly crafted bronze **uraeus**. The only element that differentiates the two statues is their wig: the statue found on the left (n°. 29) wears the **afnit**, a round headcloth that flares out towards the back leaving the shoulders uncovered; however, the statue found on the right (n°. 22), wears the **nemes**, a striped headcloth made of three sections, covering the shoulders and falling forwards on the chest. In both statues, the pharaoh is portrayed bearing a long baton (with a lotus umbel shaped stopper) in his left hand; in

his right hand he holds a mace with a pear-shaped head with concentric scales. An eight layer collar and a breastplate hang around his neck. Both are decorated with the **kheper** scarab, a hieroglyphic sign that symbolises the «future» and existence par excellence, enclosed in a **naos**.

On the buckle of the belt that holds the triangular apron of the loincloth in place the sovereign's fourth name is inscribed and surrounded by a cartouche: «*Nebkheperura*». Further down, on the loincloth itself, a column of text explains what the statue represents: «*the good god who can be trusted, the sovereign who is to be glorified, Harakhty's royal ka, Osiris, King, Lord of the Two Lands, Nebkheperura.*» The **ka** is an extremely difficult notion to explain as it cannot be related to anything we know in our culture and language. It is considered one of the spiritual elements that are essential to human personality, a manifestation of the individual's life-forces, both preservative and creative. That is, the **ka** can survive the death of the body, and becomes the deceased double and «represents» him in a certain way. After his death, the king lives in the funerary statue, called the «**ka** statue», which becomes the physical support of the deceased's **ka**: through this intermediary, rituals and offerings are presented to the ka, who now appears as an element who allows for an afterlife in the Netherworld.

A meticulous analysis of both statues has shed light on some small anomalies. The first concerns the position of the statue on the stand. Both statues usually face the same direction, however, here the statue is anchored askew on the wooden block. Although if it is leant against a wall it seems to be looking straight ahead. Unfortunately the reasons for this remain unknown. The second anomaly is more comprehensible as it has already appeared on other statues of the same type. Near the right leg, the bottom of the loincloth presents an opening of about eight inches. This was usually made to insert the funerary papyrus. After placing the papyrus inside, it was filled and blocked. *Tutankhamun's* statue presented one problem: although the orifice had been blocked using small pieces of rubble stuck together with a golden coloured plaster, there was no trace of the papyrus or of any other object.

Ka statue (n°. 29)

These statues were found in the Antechamber, facing each other on either side of the sealed doorway that led towards the Burial Chamber. Both statues represent Tutankhamun, the skin has been covered in black resin and the ornaments are gold-plated. In this statue the pharaoh is adorned with the round headgear, the afnit, and his forehead is decorated with the uraeus. He holds a baton in one hand and an item ending in a pear-shaped form in the other, both insignias of his power.

Wood coated with bitumen and gilt, with bronze, gold and glass paste elements.
Tomb n°. 62, Antechamber.
The Cairo Museum.

From the king's wardrobe to the king's «mannequin»

In his book, **Carter** refers many times to the difficulties they encountered regarding the restoration of fabrics, strips of linen or leather and the material that was found in young *Tutankhamun's* tomb. Certain clothes were found in very good condition, as if they «*had just come fresh from the loom*», others had turned to soot, given the dampness of the tomb. In these cases, it was usually impossible to save the objects in question. The great degree of deterioration was partially due to the fact that the clothing had not been treated with care in Ancient Times. During the robberies, they had been extracted from chests and thrown on the floor or left on beds. According to **Carter** it would have been better to find them in that state because the officials in charge of tidying the tomb had picked them all up, and crammed them any which way into the chests, squashing them together with all types of objects. They had decomposed due to being stored with all types of articles and scrunched into balls in chests which were generally closed.

In some cases, they had been able to treat some outfits but even then it was extremely difficult given the amount of rosettes and pearls that were sewn onto the material (especially on to the robes). According to **Carter**, some garments had been decorated with thousands of beads, hence the complexity of the task. The archaeologist recalls the case of the magnificent royal robe found in one of the chests (n°. 21) in the **Antechamber**. The material crumbled at the slightest touch, plus it was heavily decorated with faience or glass paste beads and gold pieces that had come off their settings. There were only two possible solutions: sacrifice the robe and keep the decoration, or the other way around. It seemed more reasonable to choose the first option, risk losing information regarding the size and the shape of the robe because, in **Carter's** own words, it was probably «*more important for us to keep the decorations than to have a heap of cloth and a loose handful of beads and sequins.*»

Despite the fact that not all the elements could be recovered, **Carter's** team still managed to evaluate the importance of the royal wardrobe. The clothes had not all been placed in the same chamber, initially they had been kept in chests left in the **Treasury**, the **Antechamber** and the **Annexe**. Alongside the pieces of

material whose use and shape could not be clearly identified, they did find a great amount of extraordinary articles: ceremonial outfits, robes, tunics, shirts, loincloths, coats, belts, gloves, head-cloths and cap, shawls and scarves, shoes and sandals... All of them made in bright colours and decorated with thousands of ornaments: embroidery, beads of many different sizes, golden beads, sequins, adornments... Most of these outfits were made of linen, but Carter's team also found some leather or leopard skin garments, the latter material used exclusively in the elaboration of costumes to be worn at religious ceremonies. The archaeologists were specially astounded by two types of articles: the twenty-seven gloves made using an incredibly modern technique (it was not used in the West until the Eighteenth Century), and ninety-three sandals, light sandals or shoes elaborated in such diverse materials as wickerwork (braided rush or papyrus leaves), wood or leather, all of which were sometimes decorated with varnished marquetry, beads or gold.

One cannot put an end to this chapter regarding the elements found in the **Antechamber** without mentioning an enigmatic object whose use is still not clear. This wooden bust (n°. 116), made of painted stucco wood, was found in the south wing of the **Antechamber**, near the dismantled chariots. It is cut off at the waist and its arms are missing (although this could be by accident or on purpose). Although the statue bears no inscriptions, specialists have identified it as a representation of a young *Tutankhamun*; it is an extremely realistic portrait, with plump lips and a strong protruding chin. He is wearing a unfamiliar crown, a mixture between the red crown of Lower Egypt and *Nefertiti's* high tiara, both reminiscent of Amarnian canons. As usual, his forehead is decorated with the great royal **uraeus**. The ear lobes are pierced, allowing for earrings. The body is simply painted white as if it were wearing a white shroud. Many hypotheses have been formulated regarding the nature of this object: some believe it is a ritual statue, used to carry out magic rituals to ensure the king would be born anew. Others, **Carter** among them, believe it is just a mannequin made in *Tutankhamun's* exact size, something upon which garments could be tried or fitted.

Tutankhamun's «mannequin» (n°. 116)

Although the real nature of the object is still unknown given that is bears no inscriptions, it is most probably a mannequin on which royal regalia were fitted. It depicts a young Tutankhamun, wearing a peculiar crown, reminiscent of the red crown of Lower Egypt and Nefetiti's tiara.

Stucco wood, painted and gilt. Tomb n°. 62, Antechamber. The Cairo Museum.

THE BURIAL CHAMBER
THE TOMB JEWEL...

From winter 1923 to autumn 1925

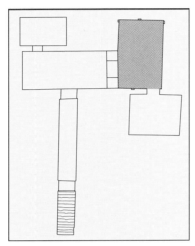

At two o'clock in the afternoon on the 17th of February 1923, more than twenty people were gathered in the tomb, awaiting the official opening of the **Burial Chamber**. The **Antechamber**, now completely empty save for the king's two protective statues on either side of the sealed doorway, had been filled with rows of seats to accommodate the guests. The audience was nervous and all had their gazes fixed on the door that would soon be knocked down, revealing if this cache, which had remained hidden for centuries, was nothing but a simple store room or the actual tomb of *Tutankhamun*. **Carter** started at the door feebly. The first thing he saw, after removing the first blocks made his hopes soar. In front of him was a golden wall which he immediately identified: it was one of the great shrines that protected the royal sarcophagus. **Carter** realised he was certainly in *Tutankhamun's* **Burial Chamber**.

Once the sealed doorway had been broken down, **Carter** entered the chamber after stopping to collect a jumble of beads he found scattered on the floor which had probably been left there by the plunderers in their hasty escape (they were part of two necklaces). The shrine was incredibly big, so much that it took up almost the whole of the chamber; there was only a space of about 23 inches between the gilt wood shrine and the walls of the chamber. Thus the difficulty to move around without damaging any of the objects on the floor. Unlike the other quarters the tomb contained, the **Burial Chamber** had an east-west orientation. It measured 20 feet 9 inches long by 13 feet 1 inch wide and held eighty nine batches, i.e. about three hundred objects that were given the catalogue numbers 172 to 260. The walls had been painted yellow and were decorated with various scenes and inscriptions. **Carter** proclaimed they were *"brilliantly coloured but had obviously been hastily crafted."* The clearing processes in the **Burial Chamber** had to be interrupted on many occasions; the first time was due to **Lord Carnarvon's** death in April 1923. However, the tomb was actually reclosed given the disagreements between **Carter** and the Egyptian Government. In fact, more than two years and a half passed between the official opening of the tomb and the autopsy of the royal mummy. As in the **Antechamber**, the objects were carried out of the Burial Chamber in a systematic order. First the objects found in the narrow passage between the outer shrine and the walls were removed, moving anticlockwise from the south-eastern angle of the chamber. Then the different shrines and the actual coffin were removed and the body was taken out.

The decoration of the sarcophagus chamber

Unlike most of the hypogeums discovered in the **Valley of the Kings**, which bear decorations and inscriptions on all their walls, only the walls of the **Burial Chamber** were decorated in *Tutankhamun's* tomb; a room referred to as the "House of Gold" or the "House of the Flesh" in the texts that recount the burial rituals. The modest size of the room was an extremely small space to illustrate the funeral of the Pharaoh, his voyage to the underworld and his heavenly rebirth. Obviously, the artists, not being able to go into great detail, had to keep to the most essential and important facts.The scenes are painted on rocky walls, covered in plaster and painted dark yellow, reminiscent of gold, the colour of *"the flesh of the gods."*

The walls are surrounded by long black strips which end in pointed tips: a hieroglyphic symbol that represents the heavens. In the lower part, a plinth, originally painted white, symbolises the ground. Unfortunately, the walls have been damaged greatly due to the dampness of the tomb: *"In many places, mainly on the decorated surfaces of the Burial Chamber, the walls were spoilt by moisture,"* **Carter** had noted. This could be caused by two factors: natural faults in the rock that allows for water to seep into the sepulchre or the precipitate closure of the vault, when the plaster on the walls was not perfectly dry. Also, speckled black marks had appeared all over the surfaces of the walls, obviously diminishing the beauty of the representations.

The sacred baboons

The western wall of the Burial Chamber (the only decorated chamber of the tomb) is ornamented with an extract from the "Book of the Amduat", i.e. the Netherworld. Here we find the twelve good genii, called the "turquoise monkeys", the first of the twelve hours of the night.

Tomb n°. 62,
Burial Chamber.
Valley of the Kings,
Western Thebes.

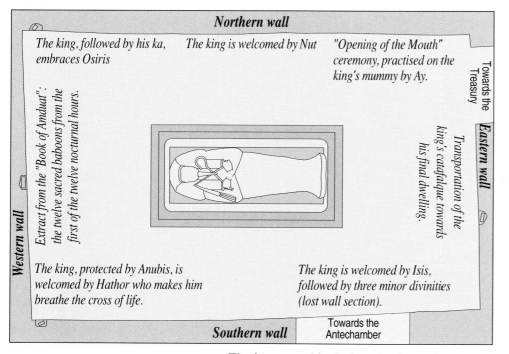

Northern wall

The king, followed by his ka, embraces Osiris

The king is welcomed by Nut

"Opening of the Mouth" ceremony, practised on the king's mummy by Ay.

Towards the Treasury

Eastern wall

Transportation of the king's catafalque towards his final dwelling.

Western wall

Extract from the "Book of Amduat": the twelve sacred baboons from the first of the twelve nocturnal hours.

The king, protected by Anubis, is welcomed by Hathor who makes him breathe the cross of life.

The king is welcomed by Isis, followed by three minor divinities (lost wall section).

Southern wall

Towards the Antechamber

Ay, the God's Father

On the northern wall of the chamber, near the passageway leading towards the Treasury, the "Opening of the Mouth" ritual is represented. It is being carried out on the mummy of the deceased by Ay, successor to Tutankhamun.. Using an adze to officiate the ceremony according to the rules, the God's Father is wearing the leopard skin, trait of priests, and crowned with the khepresh.

Tomb n°. 62,
Burial Chamber.
Valley of the Kings,
Western Thebes.

The iconographic designs begin on the eastern wall, that adjoins the **Treasury**, and represent the transportation of *Tutankhamun* towards his final dwelling. The king lies in a coffin depicted as *Osiris,* on a lion shaped bed, his name inscribed over him. The coffin has been stored inside an imposing catafalque consisting of two superposed shrines, both crowned with cobras wearing the sun disc. The ensemble is placed on a burial boat where *Isis* and *Nephthys* are also seated, watching over the deceased. The boat itself is placed on a sled pulled by twelve high officials of the royal palace. These men are clothed in white robes, white sandals and wear a white band around their foreheads, an element worn only in ceremonies of mourning. Two figures can be identified through their characteristic features: the viziers of Upper and Lower Egypt, distinguishable through their shaven heads and shoestring robes. The text inscribed over the boat haulers reflects their words: *"Nebkheperura, go in peace, oh protective god of our country."*

The northern wall represents three distinct scenes that should be looked at from right to left. In the first scene, *Ay,* the God's Father, *Tutankhamun's* successor on the Egyptian throne, is performing the "Opening of the Mouth" ritual on the mummy of the sovereign, transformed into *Osiris,* the lord of the dead. This ancient ceremony gives the deceased the power to give use to the organ with which he eats, drinks and commands; reviving his body by means of a new breath of life. On this occasion, *Ay,* whose name is inscribed over his figure, wears the priests' traditional clothing: a leopard skin and the war crown. He extends an adze to the mummy; tool without which the ceremony could not be performed. In the second scene, *Tutankhamun,* clothed as a living person, is received by *Nut,* the goddess of heaven, who invites him into the world of the gods. The last scene depicts the sovereign, followed by his **ka** (his spiritual double), embracing *Osiris,* whose body is wrapped in a mummiform sheath and his skin painted green, symbol of health and eternal youth.

The most noteworthy wall is the western side of the chamber; it is covered with images and texts extracted from the first chapter of the **"Book of the Amduat"** or **"Book of that which is in the Netherworld"**. The highest band bears a procession of five genii who walk in front of the sun boat, which bears the scarab *Khepri,* creator of life and symbol of existence par excellence. Below this, the wall is divided into twelve compartments, in three layers of four boxes. A sacred Baboon appears in each one of them, crouching and turned towards the right. They are the *"turquoise monkeys"*, benign genii from the first of the twelve hours of the night of the sun's nocturnal journey. The story of this voyage is narrated in the **"Book of Amduat"**, the **Amduat** being the Netherworld. The night is composed of twelve hours that are located along the regions that are watered by the subterranean Nile. The sun boat floats along this river, carrying the god *Ra* and his entourage, alongside the deceased sovereign. The inhabitants of the **Amduat**, the deceased, crowd the banks of the river to acclaim the sun god by the hundreds. The crew cross the twelve subterranean regions in this fashion, and their voyage is often interrupted by cosmic enemies, evil genii and other obstacles, mainly *Apophis,* the giant evil serpent, who attacks the divine boat trying sink it; although, each time he is thrown towards chaos. Finally, at dawn, *Ra* appears triumphant, depicted as *Khepri,* the rising sun, and can then initiate his diurnal voyage.

The last wall, to the south of the chamber, bears *Hathor,* goddess of the Theban necropolis, welcoming *Tutankhamun,* crowned with the **afnit** and a simple white loincloth. She makes him breathe in the **ankh,** symbol of life. *Anubis,* patron saint of embalmers, is pictured behind her, resting one hand on his back in sign of approval. Nowadays this is all that can be seen, however, the images from the archives show that when the tomb was discovered there was one other scene on the wall. To the left of the southern wall, beyond *Anubis, Isis* is depicted, followed by three minor deities, who also welcome the pharaoh to the kingdom of the deceased. **Carter's** team had to dismantle this section of the wall so as to extract the shrines from the chamber.

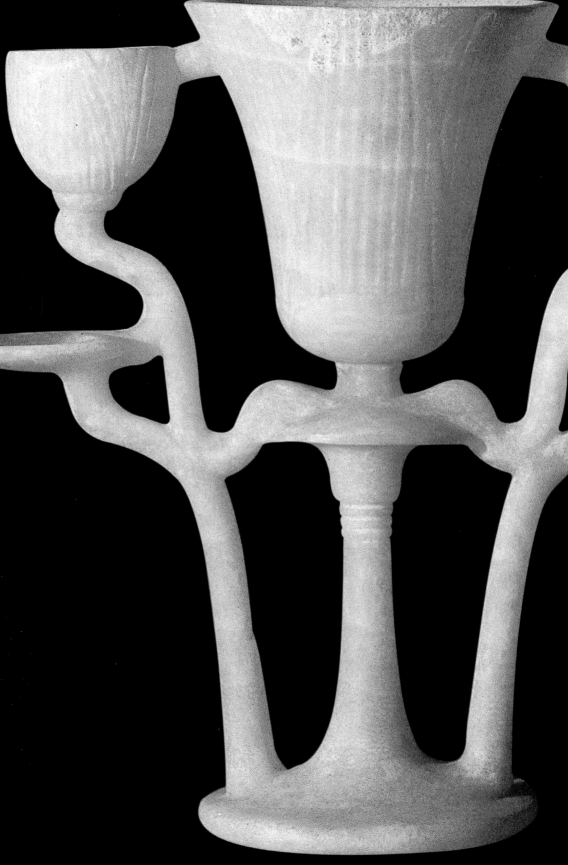

The burial shrines

In his notes, **Carter** explains how, after having made a hole in the sealed door that separated the **Antechamber** from the **Burial Chamber**, a few feet away from him, he saw *"what looked like a solid wall of gold."* He quickly realised it was the outer wall of an imposing burial shrine, through which he deduced he was actually in the chamber that held *Tutankhamun's* sarcophagus. Given that the shrine was closed, at first he could not tell what it contained; thus what he encountered was a total surprise. All in all there were four shrines, one fitted inside the other to protect the stone sarcophagus.

They were all similar in form, although progressively smaller, the shrines consisted of four big gilt cedar-wood panels, held together with a mortice and tenon joint. They were covered by a cloth, of varied shapes, and had no bottom to allow for the packing; the lower rim was covered with a sheet of copper. Towards the East, there were two heavy double doors opposite the doorway that lead to the **Treasury** which had been closed using two series of silver-plated copper rings, into which thick ebony stems had been inserted. Moreover, in the centre of each door there were two supplementary rings tied together with a thin cord bearing the seal. When the Burial Chamber was discovered, only the first seal had been opened, the ones on the two intermediary shrines were intact; regarding the innermost shrine, it had not been sealed when the king was placed within.

When the ensemble was put together, the outermost shrine took up almost all the **Burial Chamber:** *"The construction was so vast that save for a small space, it filled the chamber and stood free of each of the four walls by just twenty inches. The roof had been decorated with a cornice top and torus moulding, almost reaching the ceiling of the chamber,"* says **Carter** in his notes. Given the narrow passages that led to the chamber that held the sarcophagus, the objects had obviously been dismantled when they were brought there in ancient times and then put together once in the chamber. Thus, the same procedure had to be followed in order to extract them, but in reverse order: **Carter's** team spent eighty-four days *"of simply manual work"*, he stated, to dismantle the four structures and take them to the restoration laboratory that had been set up in the necropolis. They had approximately fifty-one pieces that weighed 100 or 150 kilos.

The first shrine (n°. 207) was 16 feet 7 inches long, 10 feet 8 inches wide, 9 feet wide and 8 feet 10 inches high. It was covered by a ridge roof, imitating the structures decorated for the royal jubilees, the **Sed Festivals**, the ceremonies that were meant to regenerate the king's physical force and his magical powers. It differs from the other shrines, as the exterior back and side walls are decorated with a motif that stands out on a blue faience background decorated alternately and repetitively with two **djed** pillars (symbol of strength and stability) and two **tit** knots (that ensure protection at all times). The interior is decorated with many formulae from the **"Book of the Dead"** and the **"Book of the Heavenly Cow"**. The ceiling is decorated with winged sun discs and vultures.

Under this first shrine, there was a wooden gilt and varnished structure (n°. 208) that held the mortuary sheet (n°. 209), a large piece of dark brown linen covered with copper daisies, which amazed the archaeologists. Then the second shrine (n°. 237) appeared under this, measuring 12 feet 3 inches long, 7 feet 7 inches wide and 7 feet 4 inches high, its form was that of **Per-wer**, *"the big house"*, name given to the original southern shrine that designated the domain of *Nekhbet*, goddess of **El-Kab** and protector of Upper Egypt. This type of structure usually has a sloping roof that rests on a grooved cornice. Apart from the scenes that depict parts of the **"Book of the Dead"** and a composition that describes the metamorphosis and triumph of the sun god, the shrine also bears two superb images on the hinges of the doors. In these, the king is protected by *Isis* and walks respectfully towards *Ra-Harakhty* and *Osiris*. The third shrine (n°. 238) resembles the aforementioned one, in the form of **Per-wer** once again; it is 11 feet 2 inches long, 6 feet 3 inches wide and 7 feet 1 inch high and is decorated with fragments from chapters II and VI of the **"Book of the Amduat"**, i.e. of the Netherworld. The innermost shrine (n°. 239) contained the sarcophagus, it was 9 feet 5 inches long, 4 feet 9 inches wide and 6 feet 2 inches high. Its top was vaulted and in the form of **Per-nu**, *"the house of the flame"*, the archaic shrine of Wadjit, the goddess of **Buto**, who protected Lower Egypt. The sides are decorated with burial deities: *Isis, Selkis, Nephthys, Neith, Anubis…*

Lamp (n° 174)

Found at the entrance of the Burial Chamber, this lamp is carved out of a single block of calcite in the shape of a triple lotus-flower emerging from the water. To light it, the cup is filled with vegetable oil and a wick of linen fibres is placed within. When Carter found the lamp, the cups still held remains of oil.

Calcite.
Tomb n°. 62,
Burial Chamber.
The Cairo Museum.

Sarcophagus and coffins

Before attempting to dismantle the burial shrines, **Carter** and his team were so eager to see what they contained that they opened the series of four doors that led to the heart of the gigantic structure: then *"an enormous sarcophagus appeared before us; made of yellow quartzite, intact, its lid still resting in place, exactly where those pious hands had deposited it."* According to **James Henry Breasted**, director of the Oriental Institute of the University of Chicago, it was at that moment when they felt the *"the real presence of the dead pharaoh"* for the first time. The rectangular sarcophagus (n°. 240) was carved from a single block of quartzite and measured 8 feet 9 inches long by 4 feet 9 inches wide. This sarcophagus and the first coffin, carefully left in its original place after being restored and analysed, are the only two treasures that remain in the tomb in the **Valley of the Kings.** The images of *Isis, Nephthys, Selkis* and *Neith* dominate the finely sculpted decorations, and appear on the four corners of the sarcophagus with wings which they spread out along the sides as a symbol of protection. The composition is completed by a text that is written in vertical lines. On the lower part, along the perimeter of the sarcophagus, **djed** pillars and **tit** knots appear alternately. The lid is adorned with three columns of text and a sun disc, although is presents some faults in its craft. In the first place, it is not carved from the same material as the sarcophagus given that it is made of pink granite, painted yellow to imitate the colour of quartzite. According to **Carter**, the real lid was not ready in time for the funeral, and it was replaced by this piece which was already cut and had probably been meant for someone else, or had just been abandoned. Also, there is a big hole in its centre which has been replastered and painted again, which archaeologists believe must have been caused by an accident when it was being lain in place; unless the split had been made at an even earlier date, which would justify it being abandoned and then recuperated for *Tutankhamun's* sarcophagus.

The stone sarcophagus was opened on the 12th of February 1924, an operation that was extremely difficult given the weight (1,250 kilos!) and, most importantly, the split in the lid: whatever happened they had to avoid that the block gave way when they lifted it, since if it fell, they risked damaging the contents of the sarcophagus.

Thus, flat angle brackets, pulleys and ropes were wisely installed to permit the procedure. The archaeologists recount how, for a few minutes, they watched the lid wobble, quiver and tremble before it moved dangerously, slowly. At first, all they could see was a big black hole, nothing precise, then, they saw a vague dark bulk that resembled the shape of a silhouette covered with a shroud. **Carter** carefully started to lift the linen cloth. At that moment the group of people in the **Burial Chamber** let out an exclamation of surprise: there before them stood a coffin gleaming in all its golden lustre!

The opening was postponed as before clearing the sarcophagus, they had to treat the items that had already been found. Thus the thorough search of the **Burial Chamber** did not start until the 10th of October 1925. The first object they analysed was the outer coffin (n°. 253); it was 7 feet 3 inches long and presented *Tutankhamun,* his head wrapped in the **afnit.** The king is represented as a recumbent effigy of Osiris, with his arms crossed over his chest, his hands holding two royal complements: the **heka** sceptre in his left hand and the flail in the right hand. On his forehead he bears the two protective symbols of Egypt: the *Wadjit* cobra of the North and *Nekhbet* the vulture from the South. The coffin, made of cypress wood, is covered with layer of gold of different densities: it is quite thick on the head and hands, but the head-cloth has only been given a thin coating. A **"rishi"** type decoration is sculpted along the whole surface of the body, rishi being the feather-based motifs that became popular in the 17th Dynasty and were still used on members of the royal family during the 18th Dynasty. Under his arms, are the images of *Isis* and *Nephthys,* both of whom protect the late king with their outstretched wings. The image of *Isis* appears again on the lower part of the lid, at the sovereign's feet: kneeling on a **nub** sign, representing gold, she opens her winged arms over *Tutankhamun* and watches over him as she formerly watched over *Osiris*. The lid was attached to the coffin by ten strips of solid silver: four on each side, one at his feet and one at his head; all kept in place with thick nails, also made of precious metal. To hoist the lid, first they had to take out the nails, a task which proved extremely delicate as the coffin filled almost all of the inner part of the sarcophagus.

TUTANKHAMUN'S BURIAL CHAMBER

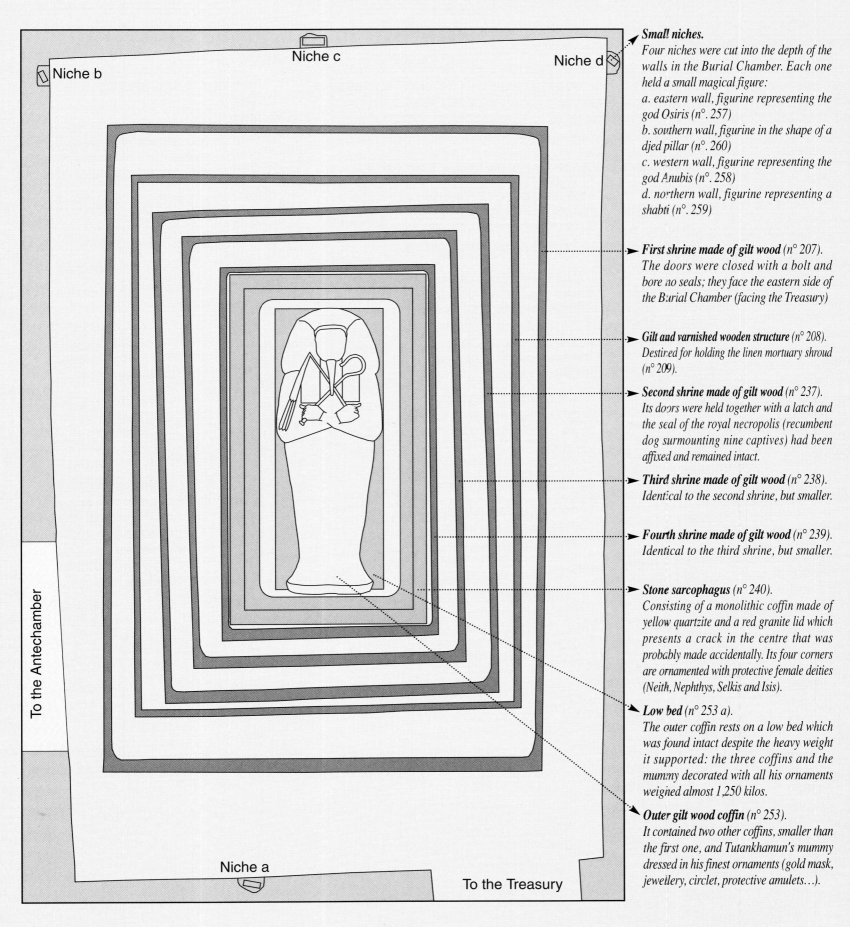

Small niches.
Four niches were cut into the depth of the walls in the Burial Chamber. Each one held a small magical figure:
a. eastern wall, figurine representing the god Osiris (n°. 257)
b. southern wall, figurine in the shape of a djed pillar (n°. 260)
c. western wall, figurine representing the god Anubis (n°. 258)
d. northern wall, figurine representing a shabti (n°. 259)

First shrine made of gilt wood (n° 207). The doors were closed with a bolt and bore no seals; they face the eastern side of the Burial Chamber (facing the Treasury)

Gilt and varnished wooden structure (n° 208). Destined for holding the linen mortuary shroud (n° 209).

Second shrine made of gilt wood (n° 237). Its doors were held together with a latch and the seal of the royal necropolis (recumbent dog surmounting nine captives) had been affixed and remained intact.

Third shrine made of gilt wood (n° 238). Identical to the second shrine, but smaller.

Fourth shrine made of gilt wood (n° 239). Identical to the third shrine, but smaller.

Stone sarcophagus (n° 240). Consisting of a monolithic coffin made of yellow quartzite and a red granite lid which presents a crack in the centre that was probably made accidentally. Its four corners are ornamented with protective female deities (Neith, Nephthys, Selkis and Isis).

Low bed (n° 253 a). The outer coffin rests on a low bed which was found intact despite the heavy weight it supported: the three coffins and the mummy decorated with all his ornaments weighed almost 1,250 kilos.

Outer gilt wood coffin (n° 253). It contained two other coffins, smaller than the first one, and Tutankhamun's mummy dressed in his finest ornaments (gold mask, jewellery, circlet, protective amulets...).

Niche c

Niche b

Niche d

To the Antechamber

Niche a

To the Treasury

The lid was also adorned with four silver handles, that had been used to ensure it was placed correctly.. If they were to be used to lift the lid, first they had to be inspected to examine their state of preservation and avoid any incidents. **Carter** analysed them meticulously and deemed they were strong enough to hold the weight of the lid. The operation was set in motion: once the winch and pulleys were set in place they could begin. *"It was a moment of intense emotion and extreme anxiety,"* says **Carter.** The lid was lifted effortlessly, revealing another coffin covered in a linen shroud, in a bad state of preservation, on top of which flower garlands had been lain. Multicoloured incrustations could be seen through the material, in some places it seemed as if they were about to come loose from their supports. There was obviously some kind of dampness inside the coffin. It was then that they decided to lift the whole structure out of the quartzite coffin; the whole consisting of the second coffin (which was still closed) and the body of the first one. Despite the heaviness of the objects (they weighed over a ton), the task was carried out without too much trouble and the precious parcel was left on some trestles that had been placed at the end of the sarcophagus.

The second coffin (n°. 254) was 6 feet 7 inches long and also made of wood. However, it was different from the first coffin given the thickness of the gold coating and the amount of incrustations that covered it. It also depicted the pharaoh as *Osiris,* with the cobra and the vulture on his forehead, the false beard of the gods and his arms crossed over his chest holding the royal complements. Only a few details are altered: here *Tutankhamun* is not wearing the **afnit** but the striped **nemes**; the **rishi** decoration that covers the body is totally inlaid with coloured glass simulating jasper, turquoise and lapis lazuli. On this occasion the figures of *Nekhbet* and *Wadjit* replace *Isis* and *Nephthys* adorning his body.

After a hasty analysis, **Carter** realised how difficult it would be to extract this coffin. To begin with, no handles had been affixed to it, which meant that the whole coffin would have to be lifted without removing its lid. Also, it was so closely inserted into the first coffin –there was barely a space of 0.2 inches between them– that it was impossible to slide ropes or any other lifting instrument underneath it. Another factor was the fragility of the inlays and the weight of the coffin. Albeit dangerous, the solution they adopted was successful: they decided to unscrew the nails that secured the strips

of the lid a few millimetres, and attached solid strips of copper to them. They also decided to place some metallic grommets on the edge of the first coffin. Then, the whole ensemble was tied with ropes that were put into action by the pulleys. The two coffins came apart, not because the second one was lifted out but because the first sank into the stone sarcophagus. For a few seconds, the intermediate coffin hung suspended in mid-air, supported only by the strips of copper. They quickly placed a wooden plank underneath the sarcophagus so as to lay it there. They still had to open the coffin, thus they unscrewed the support nails and using the grommets placed on its four corners and a winch, the lid finally moved. A third coffin appeared, also similar to the first two. The body was covered with a dark linen cloth and a floral collar, the **nemes** was concealed under a thin fabric. In fact, only the head-part was visible.

The third coffin (n°. 255) was noteworthy for its craftsmanship, not what it represented. **Carter** recounts that the vision of the coffin was *"astounding"* because... *"it was made of solid gold."* There were exactly 110.4 kilos of gold along the length of the coffin (6 feet 2 inches) and the gold coating was approximately 0.1 inches thick. Apart from the decorations that had been carved on the actual coffin (images of *Isis* and *Nephthys* on the body, the **rishi** feathers and the **nemes** stripes), another decoration stood out: plates of cloisonné gold representing the deities *Nekhbet* and *Wadjit,* with bodies inlaid with quartz and blue glass, with outstretched wings that protect the king. A double collar is placed around the neck, consisting of yellow and red gold and blue faience discs; the arms are decorated with multicoloured bracelets, in turquoise, lapis lazuli and carnelian. Despite the beauty of the object, **Carter** was still anxious; this sparkling decoration was hidden under *"a black glistening coating produced by the ointments that had been poured over the coffin."* Moreover, the product had spread and had finally filled the space that was left between the two coffins; with time it had become solidified and had welded the two pieces together. For the moment, **Carter** decided not to extract the third coffin from the body of the second one, thinking it was better to start by simply opening it. The lid was secured by eight golden tenons, held in place by long solid gold nails. After extracting them, they pulled on the four handles: *"Lying there in front of us,"* says **Carter,** *"was a stunning mummified body, clean and immaculate."*

Intermediate coffin (n° 254)

This coffin, decorated with a feather-based rishi decoration on the body, depicts the king as Osiris. He wears a striped nemes and the cobra Nekhbet and the vulture Wadjit (the two protective deities of Egypt) appear on his forehead. He is holding the symbols of power: the heka cross and the nekhakha flail.

Gilt wood inlaid
with glass paste.
Tomb n°. 62,
Burial Chamber.
The Cairo Museum.

Mask and ornaments

After they had recovered from their amazement, **Carter** and his team started to inspect the mummy in more detail. *"Among the dark blackish shades, we could make out the gold mask made in the pharaoh's image, sparkling and beautiful,"* wrote **Carter.** Although the embalmers had coated the body with a great amount of ointment and then wrapped it in a linen shroud, they had taken great care not to stain the burial mask (n°. 256a) that was placed over the pharaoh's face. This unique mask was 21 inches high and weighed 10.23 kilos. It represents *Tutankhamun* as Osiris, his head wrapped in the **nemes** and his chin adorned with the false beard. His forehead bears the two deities of Egypt: *Nekhbet* the vulture for the South and *Wadjit,* the cobra, for the North. A breastplate with two falcon heads on the ends hangs from his neck. The back part bears excerpts from the **"Book of the Dead".** The mask consists of two gold plates that are beaten together; the richness of the glass, faience or precious stones inlays is incredible. In particular, his eyes are very well-accomplished: the eyeball is made of quartz, the iris of obsidian, even the caroncle appears in the inner angle of the eyelids, represented with small red speckles. The setting of the eyes and the eyebrows are depicted with a fine lapis lazuli incrustations.

Beneath the false beard, a three-string necklace with layers of beads made of yellow or red gold and faience has been attached to the mask. However, given the density of the ointment that covered the mummy, it was difficult to make out the other elements that covered it. Some other articles were found, but none were in a good state of preservation. His hands have been replaced by two golden hands that are crossed over the chest and hold the **heka** sceptre, and the flail (n°. 256b[1]) had been sewn onto the shroud. A scarab made of dark resin (n°. 256b) had been placed between them and affixed to the neck by long golden straps. Flexible strips surrounded his legs; they were made of gold with inlaid glass and semi-precious stones: a long vertical strip (n°. 256b[4]) went along the length of the ribcage; four horizontal strips (n°. 256b[3]) were placed perpendicularly at regular distances. The bird **ba** with outstretched wings (n°. 256b[2]), symbol of the soul, appeared at the top of the frame. In the first place they took all the adornments off the mummy, in order to assess the amount of damage the ointment had caused inside the coffin. The result came as a bolt from the blue: the acids from the ointment had blackened the bandages and, more importantly, the blackish solidified glue has stuck the mummy and the mask to the coffin. They had to find a way to melt the solution without damaging the skin and the treasures it bore. **Carter** decided to use heat, and at first thought the sun would be hot enough to soften the substance. However, it did not help at all, despite the amount of hours of exposure. Although it was a good idea, a greater degree of heat was needed to carry the chore out successfully. The next decision was to submit the ensemble to a temperature of 932°F using paraffin lamps placed under the coffins, which was protected by thick plates of zinc and wet covers. After a few hours, they managed to loosen the different elements which were then taken to the restoration laboratory. The only thing left in the **Burial Chamber** was the first coffin which was placed back inside the stone sarcophagus once the preliminary manipulations had been carried out. It was moved easily by means of a winch. A low lion-shaped bed made of gilt wood (n°. 253a) was found at the bottom of the coffin, perfectly preserved despite the weight it had been supporting all the years (around 1.250 kilos).

The unravelling of the mummy's bandages revealed one hundred and four batches of objects (nos. 256c to 256-4v) as well as the gold mask and the outer ornaments. The king's body was decorated with more than one hundred and forty jewels, amulets or other ornaments that were to ensure his immortality. All these had been placed on his body meticulously following the indications from the **"Book of the Dead".** For example, in the chapter CLVI titled "To affix a carnelian talisman" it says: *"This chapter shall be recited over a carnelian loop, which will have lain in the water of Ankham flowers, inlaid in a sycamore-wood tablet. On the day of the funeral, this tablet shall be placed around the deceased's neck. Once this had been done, the powers of Isis will protect the limbs of the deceased; Horus, son of Isis, will rejoice when seeing him at the centre of the mysteries of the path, with one arm outstretched towards the heavens and the other towards the earth; forever, eternally. Never let a single person see this text, ever"* (**tit** knot amulet n° 256fff).

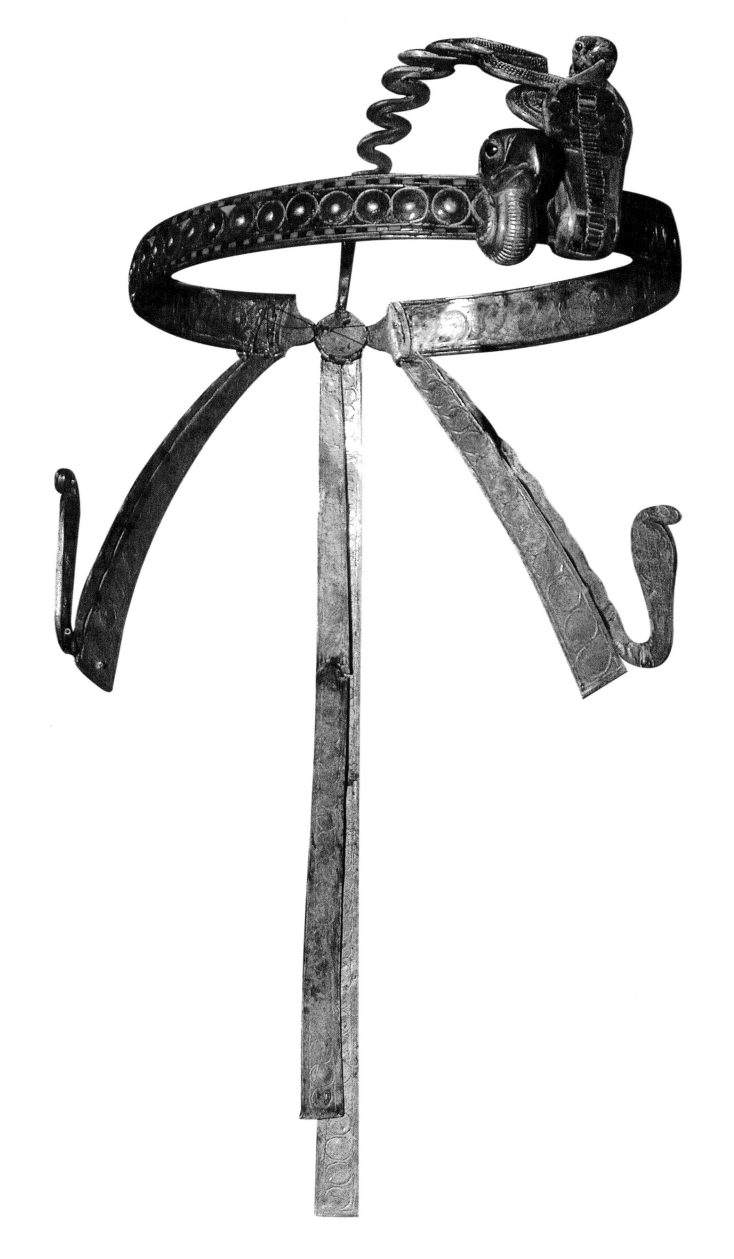

Inventory of adornments found on Tutankhamun's mummy

N°	OBJET	EMPLACEMENT
256a	*Tutankhamun's* gold mask (inlaid gold)	over the face
256b	Scarab (black resin)	on the mummy's shroud, between the gold hands
256b[1]	Two hands holding the **heka** sceptre and the **nekhakha** flail (gold)	sewn onto the shroud, instead of hands
256b[2]	**Ba** bird, with outstretched wings symbolising the soul (gold)	on the mummy's shroud, directly under the golden hands
256b[3]	Four small flexible horizontal strips (inlaid gold)	on the mummy's shroud, on the lower part of the body
256b[4]	Flexible vertical strip (inlaid gold)	on the mummy's shroud, on the lower part of the body
256c	Inverted Y-shaped amulet, representing the hieroglyph of the tissue (gold)	on the left side of the mummy
256d	Oval-shaped plate (gold)	placed on the left side of the mummy where an incision was made to extract the viscera
256e	Breastplate adorned with the *Nekhbet* vulture with outstretched wings (incised gold)	between the neck and the waist, first pendant
256f	"Nebti" breastplate, decorated with the cobra and the vulture (incised gold)	between the neck and the waist, second pendant
256g	Breastplate decorated with the *Wadjit* cobra with outstretched wings (incised gold)	between the neck and the waist, third pendant
256h	Breastplate with two falcon heads at its tips (incised gold)	between the neck and the waist, fourth pendant
256i	Two collars decorated with a falcon (cloisonné gold)	on the tibias
256j	Rectangular loincloth with twenty layers of beads (gold, faience and glass)	on the legs
256k	Iron bladed dagger ending in a rock crystal knob	laying on the right thigh
256l	Thin flexible belt (gold)	around the waist
256m	T-shaped amulet (gold)	on the left part of the waist
256n	Large bracelet (gold)	in the hollow of the left groin
256o	Long bead necklace (dark blue faience)	on the left side of the waist
256p	Breastplate decorated with the *Horus* falcon (incised gold)	between the neck and the waist, sixth pendant
256q	Scarab-shaped pendant amulet (black resin)	between the neck and the waist, fifth pendant
256r	*Wadjit* cobra from the royal circlet n°. 256-4o (cloisonné gold)	along the right thigh
256s	*Nekhbet* vulture from the royal circlet n°. 256-4o (cloisonné gold)	on the right knee, near the blade of dagger n° 256k
256t	Breastplate decorated with the *Horus* falcon, known as the "*Horus*" necklace" (gold)	on top of the five layers of pendants placed around the neck
256u	Bracelet (gold and glass)	on the waist
256v	Round ring (gold)	on the right thigh
256w	Round ring (gold)	on the left thigh
256x	Bracelet decorated with the *Nekhbet* vulture (inlaid gold)	first bracelet on the right fore-arm
256y	Series of pearls	on the left thigh
256z	Breastplate decorated with the *Horus* falcon, known as the "*Horus*" necklace" (cloisonné gold)	between the neck and the waist, seventh pendant
256aa	Two collars decorated with a falcon (cloisonné gold)	on the knees
256bb	String of pearls	at waist level, near dagger n° 256dd
256cc	Round ring (gold) (or)	on the genitals
256dd	Gold bladed dagger, handle decorated with granulations (cloisonné gold)	on belt n°. 256ee, to the right of the waist, the blade facing left
256ee	Thin flexible belt (made of gold)	around the waist
256ff	Five ring-seals (gold and precious stones)	on the right wrist
256gg	Breastplate decorated with two falcons on its ends (gold and glass)	between the neck and the waist, sixteenth pendant
256hh(1)	Bracelet (gold threads) decorated with a drum-shaped bead (lapis lazuli)	on the left fore-arm
256hh(2)	Bracelet (gold threads) decorated with a **wedjat**-eye (iron)	on the left fore-arm
256hh(3)	Bracelet (gold threads) decorated with a drum-shaped bead (carnelian)	on the left fore-arm
256ii	Fragments of burial papyrus	between the amulets hanging from the neck
256jj	Four round rings (gold)	spread out longways from the waist to the knees
256kk	**Djed** pillar-shaped pendant amulet	around the neck (second pendant from the second range)
256ll	Sandals and fingerstalls (gold)	sandals on feet and fingerstalls at the tips of fingers and toes
256mm	Bracelet (metallic threads?)	not stated
256nn	Pearl-embroidery surrounding the ritual stalk n° 256eee	under the mummy, affixed to belt n° 256ee
256oo	Bracelet decorated with an openwork **wedjat**-eye pattern (inlaid gold)	second bracelet on the right fore-arm
256pp	Bracelet decorated with a jasper **wedjat**-eye near the clasp (inlaid gold)	third bracelet on the right fore-arm
256qq	Flexible bracelet with scarab and cobra decorations (inlaid gold)	fourth bracelet on the right fore-arm
256rr	Bracelet with drum-shaped beads (inlaid gold)	fifth bracelet on the right fore-arm
256ss	Flexible pearl bracelet with scarab and cobra decorations in green stone (inlaid gold)	sixth bracelet on the right fore-arm
256ss bis	Bracelet with a rectangular precious stone in the centre (inlaid gold)	seventh bracelet on the right fore-arm

N°	OBJET	EMPLACEMENT
256tt	Amulet in the shape of the god's magic knot (gold)	at the same level as the straps that surround amulet n°. 256kkk and breastplate n°. 256gg.
256uu	Bracelet decorated with a swallow (gold and carnelian)	near the left elbow
256vv	Eight ring-seals (gold and precious stones)	between the left wrist and the right fore-arm.
256ww	Bracelet with drum-shaped beads (inlaid gold)	second bracelet on the left fore-arm
256xx	Bead bracelet (inlaid gold)	third bracelet on the left fore-arm
256yy	Flexible bracelet with scarab and cobra decorations (inlaid gold)	fourth bracelet on the left fore-arm
256zz	Bracelet decorated with a **wedjat**-eye (inlaid gold)	fifth bracelet on the left fore-arm
256aaa	Bracelet decorated with an openwork **wedjat**-eye pattern (inlaid gold)	sixth bracelet on the left fore-arm
256bbb	Signet ring (gold)	on the fingerstall, on the left middle finger.
256ccc	Signet ring (gold)	on the fingerstall, on the left ring finger.
256ddd	Bracelet with a rectangular precious stone in the centre (inlaid gold)	first bracelet on the left fore-arm
256eee	Ritual stalk covered with pearl embroidery n°. 256nn	under the mummy, on belt n°. 256ee
256fff	**Tit** knot-shaped pendant amulet (gold and carnelian)	around the neck (first pendant of the second range)
256ggg	**Wadj** column-shaped pendant amulet (gold)	around the neck (third pendant of the second range)
256hhh	**Djed** pillar-shaped pendant amulet (gold and faience)	around the neck (fourth pendant of the second range)
256iii	Oblong double leaf-shaped pendant amulet (gold)	around the neck (first pendant of the second range)
256iii bis	Snake-shaped pendant amulet (gold)	around the neck (second pendant of the second range)
256jjj	Oblong leaf-shaped pendant amulet (gold)	around the neck (third pendant of the second range)
256kkk	Pending amulet in the shape of the god's magic knot	around the neck at the same level as the straps that surround breastplate n°. 256gg and amulet n°. 256tt
256lll	Collar decorated with the cobra *Wadjit* (cloisonné gold)	between the neck and the waist, ninth pendant
256mmm	Collar decorated with the vulture *Nekhbet* with outstretched wings (cloisonné gold)	between the neck and the waist, eighth pendant
256nnn	Collar decorated with the cobra *Wadjit* and the vulture *Nekhbet* (cloisonné gold)	between the neck and the waist, tenth pendant
256ooo	Necklace decorated with three sun scarabs (gold and lapis lazuli)	between the neck and the waist, twelfth pendant
256ppp	Necklace decorated with the vulture *Nekhbet* with folded wings	between the neck and the waist, eleventh pendant
256qqq	Necklace decorated with a winged scarab (cloisonné gold)	between the neck and the waist, thirteenth pendant
256rrr	**Wedjat**-eye pendant amulet (blue faience)	around the waist, on belt n°. 256sss
256sss	Thin flexible beaded belt (gold and faience)	around the waist
256ttt	Necklace decorated with a falcon	not mentioned
256uuu	Necklace decorated with a sun falcon with outstretched wings (cloisonné gold)	between the neck and the waist, fourteenth pendant
256vvv	Necklace decorated with a **wedjat**-eye surrounded by the vulture and the cobra (cloisonné gold)	between the neck and the waist, fifteenth pendant
256www	Bracelet decorated with six **wadjet** eyes (gold and green glass)	near the right elbow
256xxx	Pendant amulet in the form of the jackal *Anubis* (gold and faience)	around the neck (fourth pendant of the third range)
256yyy	Pendant amulet in the form of *Horus* the falcon (gold and faience)	around the neck (third pendant of the third range)
256zzz	Snake-shaped pendant amulet (gold and carnelian)	around the neck (second pendant of the third range)
256-4a	Pendant amulet in the form of the ibis *Thoth* (gold and faience)	around the neck (first pendant of the third range)
256-4b	**Wadj** column-shaped pendant amulet (gold and feldspar)	around the neck (fifth pendant of the third range)
256-4c	Pearl	not mentioned
256-4d	Chain	not mentioned
256-4e	Five breastplate clasps and pendants	not mentioned
256-4f	Pendant amulet shaped as a winged **uraeus** with human head (incised gold)	around the neck (first pendant of the fourth range)
256-4g	Pendant amulet shaped as a double **uraeus** (incised gold)	around the neck (second pendant of the fourth range)
256-4h	Vulture-shaped pendant amulet (incised gold)	around the neck (third pendant of the fourth range)
256-4i	Vulture-shaped pendant amulet (incised gold)	around the neck (first pendant of the fourth range)
256-4i bis	Vulture-shaped pendant amulet (incised gold)	around the neck (second pendant of the fourth range)
256-4j	Vulture-shaped pendant amulet (incised gold)	around the neck (third pendant of the fourth range)
256-4k	**Uraeus**-shaped pendant amulet (incised gold)	around the neck (fourth pendant of the fourth range)
256-4l	Vulture-shaped pendant amulet (incised gold)	around the neck (fifth pendant of the fourth range)
256-4m	Necklace with four layers of round beads	around the neck
256-4n	Two hairnets (fibre and string)	on the mummified head, directly under the gold mask n°. 256a
256-4o	Royal circlet (gold inlaid with carnelian and glass)	on the head, on the headband n°. 256-4p
256-4p	Headband stretched over both temple covering the eyes(gold)	destined for supporting the head-dress n°. 256-4p bis, over both temples
256-4p bis	Head-cloth finishing in a tail at the back (linen)	on the head, above the cloth n°. 256-4t
256-4q	*Wadjit* cobra-shaped insignia (inlaid gold)	on the head, decorating head-cloth n°. 256-4p bis
256-4r	**Nekhbet** vulture-shaped insignia(inlaid gold)	on the head, decorating head-cloth n°. 256-4p bis
256-4s	Headband stretching between both temples (gold)	meant to support cloth n°. 256-4t, covering both temples and the forehead.
256-4t	Cloth decorated at the top with four cobras (linen with gold and faience pearls)	placed directly on the shaven head
256-4u	Conical small cushion	under the nape of the neck
256-4v	Bedhead amulet (iron)	under the nape of the neck

Chapter CLV, entitled "To attach a gold **djed** pillar" explains how to carry out this procedure: *"This chapter shall be recited over a gold djed pillar placed in sycamore wood that had been placed in the water of Ankham flowers. On the day of the funeral, place said djed pillar around the deceased's neck. Thus, in the underworld, he will become a saintly perfect spirit; and on New Year's day, he will assimilate the spirits of Osiris' entourage, truly, forever, eternally"* (**djed** pillar amulet n°. 256hhh).

Thus when bandaging, the officials had placed the jewels in superimposed layers, each of them separated by and wrapped in a few linen bandages. The neck was the most protected part of the body and was covered by two layers of ornaments given that it was considered the support of the body that was the means of reanimation. The first layer actually covered the king's neck, the second was between the neck and the waist. In total there were thirty-eight pendant amulets, necklaces, golden collars or breastplates, either incised, cloisonné or inlaid with precious stones, faience or glass paste. Many of these jewels are shaped in the form of the *Horus* falcon, who protected royalty, or the "Two Ladies", main deities of Upper and Lower Egypt: the vulture *Nekhbet* from the South and the cobra **Wadjit** from the North. However other deities such as *Thoth* as an ibis and *Anubis* as a jackal also appear alongside hieroglyphic symbols charged with magical forces: **djed** pillars, symbolising strength and stability, the **tit** knot, guaranteeing the protection of *Isis,* the **Wadj** column, ensuring vigour, fertility and eternal youth, and the **wadjet** eye, giving health, integrity and plenitude.

The fore-arms were also decorated with seven bracelets on his right arm and six on the left; all of which were made of inlaid gold. Although some are only decorated with beads and no stones, others are adorned with the **wadjet** eye (symbolising integrity and plenitude) or the **kheper** scarab (symbolising existence and rebirth). Officials had also placed objects on the elbows and wrists and between the crossed arms; these were ring-seals bearing *Tutankhamun's* name, gold bracelets inlaid with precious stones and thin gold-thread bracelets, two of which bore one bead made of lapis lazuli and one of carnelian, and another a **wadjet** eye made of iron, a material that was barely known in Egypt in this era. By the straps there were two gold magic knots, amulets that imitate the thin knotted cords the gods used to carry.

Three belts were wound around the pharaoh's waist. Some had other objects attached to them, for example a superb dagger with a gold blade and sheath. The handle is adorned with small granulated incrustations, made of gold, semi-precious stones or glass paste; the sheath depicts a hunting scene with dogs and tame cheetahs and lions attacking a pack of wild animals. An oval plate and a overturned Y-shaped amulet, that evokes the hieroglyph of the tissue, have been placed over the left flank to cover the incision made by the embalmers to extract the internal organs. Various objects have been placed on either side of the waist, notably a long necklace made of blue faience beads (imitating lapis lazuli) and a series of gold bracelets that are spread out towards the knees. The genitals are also covered by a rectangular loincloth with twenty layers of beads that is surrounded by the "Two Ladies" that were initially placed on the royal circlet: on the right thigh, facing southwards, *Nekhbet* the vulture and on the left thigh, facing northwards, *Wadjit* the cobra. The reasons for dismantling these superb cloisonné gold elements from the jewel when mummifying the body are unknown. It could have been part of the ritual or just a decision taken by the embalmers so as to limit the saturation of the head, which had to bear the gold mask on top of so many layers of ornaments. Whatever the case, the priests decided to place these items here, respecting the orientation attributed to the deities. The officials had placed another dagger on the right thigh, pressed against the vulture from the circlet; this one is even more astounding than the first: firstly, the blade is made of iron (an extremely rare material in Egypt in this era) but also its handle ends in a big rock crystal knob. The fingers and toes are covered with gold fingerstalls and the middle and ring finger are decorated with a gold signet ring engraved with *Tutankhamun's* name. The feet are covered with gilt sandals.

In contrast to the royal mummies from the 18th Dynasty found in the **Deir el-Bahri** cache, Tutankhamun's head had been shaved and was covered with many head-cloths and ornaments: first a linen cloth decorated with beads and four cobras bearing cartouches with the name of the sun disc Aten, held in place by a gold headband. Then a linen head-cloth ending in a tail at the back, held in place by another headband with gold representations of Nekhbet and Wadjit of gold. The last object was the circlet, an incredible jewel made of a gold hoop inlaid with carnelian discs.

Gold blade dagger (n° 256dd)

Found on the mummy at waist level, under a gold belt, this dagger with a gold blade and sheath is a masterpiece of goldsmith's art. The handle is also made of gold and decorated with geometric designs and flower motifs inlaid with fine stones and multicoloured glass paste elements. Various vertical grooves run along the blade, composing a stem surmounted by a small floral palmettes.

Cloisonné and granulated gold, inlaid with precious stones and glass paste.
Tomb n°. 62,
Burial Chamber.
The Cairo Museum.

83

The royal mummy

The autopsy of young *Tutankhamun's* body was performed in two phases: from the 11th to the 15th of November 1925 the preliminary examination was carried out, whilst the body was still inside the inner coffin and the head was still covered by the gold mask. It was not until the 16th of November, when the body was finally removed from the coffin, that it underwent a deeper analysis. **Howard Carter**, the restorer **Alfred Lucas** and the photographer **Harry Burton** were at the scene alongside many Egyptian and European personalities who had come for the occasion and the practitioners **Dr. Saleh Bey Hamdi** (doctor in **Alexandria**) and **Dr. Douglas E. Derry**, professor of anatomy at the Egyptian University of **Cairo**.

The external aspect of the mummified body was quite disheartening: the resins and ointments that had been spread thickly over the body had blackened the cloths and, in some places, they had become so hard that it was impossible to extract the king from his coffin or to remove the gold mask from his face. Thus, during the first phase of the analysis, the mummy had to be studied in the state it was found. First an incision was made in the torso, in order to reach the less damaged regions which could shed some light on the technique the embalmers had used to bandage the sovereign's body. The results were not too decisive: the bandages were all crumbling, expect in localised places; they could not tell precisely whether the king had received the traditional embalming process. Thankfully, the golden fingerstalls had protected the limbs, which were in better condition than the rest of the body. Through them, they noted that the embalmers had followed the bandaging method that was used in the New Kingdom: first, each finger was embalmed individually, then each limb, then the whole body.

The sovereign was lying with his legs side by side and his arms crossed over his chest, the left on top of the right hand. When analysing the genitals they noted that the penis was erect, although they could not tell if the king had been circumcised according to traditional rites, and the scrotum was crushed against the perineum. The absence of pubic hair indicates the king was shaved or depilated before being embalmed. The incision performed on the left side of the body to extract internal organs, had not been made in the traditional section nor followed traditional characteristics: it was 3 inches long, it was made in a more central position, began at the navel and stretched diagonally towards the bone of the left hip.

Upon reaching this stage of the autopsy, they decided to remove the mummy from the coffin, an extremely difficult operation given the amount of hardened resin: *"As it was impossible to continue the task of removing the objects that still covered the thorax and the top part of the body, we decided to remove the lower limbs and, finally, cut across the body directly over the hip bones, given that these were firmly welded to the coffin. After doing this, the lower part of the torso was removed,"* explains **Dr. Derry.** Thus, in order to extract the body it had to be severed in three sections: pelvis and lower limbs, upper torso and upper limbs, head and neck. The gold mask still posed a serious problem as the resin and ointments had literally welded to the face, *"we finally succeeded using knives that had been exposed to heat before they were used,"* recalls **Carter.** Thus after having removed the gold mask and the different ornaments found among the layers of bandages, *Tutankhamun's* face finally appeared. The scalp had been shaven (following priestly tradition), then covered in a thick white balm. All orifices (nostrils, inside the skull and the eyes) had been filled with cloths impregnated in gumma. The lips had also been sealed with a thin layer of resin. The nose had been involuntarily broken by a bandage tied too tightly around the head.

Dr. Derry concluded that *Tutankhamun* was a young man of short height, only 5 feet 5 inches tall, and he most probably had frail health. On the day of his funeral he must have been between the age of seventeen and nineteen maximum. These results were confirmed by a second analysis carried out on the mummy in 1968 by a British expedition from the University of Liverpool, lead by professor **Harisson**. Unfortunately, the latter died before he could publish his findings, however, the observations of one of his associates (**F. Filce Leek**) were published in 1972. This report and the x-rays that were presented with it determined that the mummy presented various anomalies: many missing ribs and sternum, many broken bones...

Also some Egyptologists formulated the hypothesis that the death had been caused by an accident linked to a fall from a chariot or a similar situation. However, before considering this assumption, one must bear in mind that **Dr. Derry's** team had broken the mummy into three pieces before removing it from the coffin. In all truth, the cause of *Tutankhamun's* premature death is unknown: illness, accident or murder? Apart from the theory of the fall, there was also that of tuberculosis being the reason of his death, although today this hypothesis has been rejected after having analysed the x-rays which show that the epiphysis were intact at vertebra level. The murder theory, which is more and more often believed, came about from the wound noted on the skull which could have been made by a violent blow to his left temple. However, to this day, none of these hypotheses has been seriously or scientifically proven.

The most interesting aspect of the analysis carried out on the royal mummy was that which compared it to the skull found in tomb n°. 55. This tomb was found in 1907 to the north-east of *Tutankhamun's* vault by an archaeologist working in **Theodore Davis'** team and to this day is still mysterious given that the identity of its occupant is still unknown. It was composed of a single passage that lead to a single chamber containing diverse eclectic objects: a gilt wood shrine, four Canopic jars, various figurines and, most importantly, a mummy in its coffin. **Davis** believed it was the tomb of *Akhenaten's* mother, as he states in his book *"The tomb of queen Tiy."* After a few years and a few studies had been performed (mostly on the mummy), the researchers stated it was a male body, and *Akhenaten's* name was mentioned straightaway. However, the discovery of *Tutankhamun's* tomb would modify these theories. In 1968, professor **Harisson's** team noted there was an uncanny similitude between the bodies of the young king and the one found in the anonymous tomb. A series of medical examinations were carried out in order to compare the two mummies: they started by measuring their skulls, and then analysed their blood group. The results were positive and led the scientists to conclude that the occupant was a brother or half-brother of *Tutankhamun*, undoubtedly *Smenekhkara*, princess *Meritaten's* husband, eldest daughter of *Akhenaten* and queen *Nefertiti*.

MUMMIFICATION

Egyptian belief did not consider death as an end but as a passage towards another form of existence. This passage is very dangerous given that, after death, the different elements of the individual's personality become dispersed, although they all keep their individual integrity. The second life will only be reached if they can all be joined anew. Thus, it is extremely important to care for the most fragile element: the body. If it is left to decompose, it will be robbed of all chance of survival. Embalming is the method through which the body can be conserved correctly. This operation, performed by specialists, is well known through the writings of **Herodotus** (a Greek traveller who visited Egypt circa 450 B.C.)

"First they extracted part of the brain through the nostrils using an iron hook, the other part was dissolved using various drugs. Then, using a sharp stone, they make an incision along one side and empty the body of all the internal organs; thus, when the insides are clean they pass palm-tree wine through it and perfume it with aromatic substances. They then fill the stomach with pure ground myrrh, cassia and other well-known aromas, all except incense. Finally, they resew it." All that was left were the skin, bones and cartilage which had to be dehydrated to avoid deterioration.

"They covered the body with salt by submerging it in natron for seventy days. After these seventy days, they cleaned the mummy and bandaged it completely with very thin gauze and coated with the gumma the Egyptians use instead of glue." At times, the bandages were hundreds of metres long, each limb was individually wrapped before bandaging the whole of the body. During the application of these cloths, the official inserted protective amulets in the places mentioned in the **"Book of the Dead"**: the **wadjet**-eye, **djed** pillar, **tit** knot, gold fingerstalls... The heart is set into its place anew once the mummification has been performed. The internal organs are treated separately, following the same technique, and then placed in the four Canopic jars which are protected by the *four sons of Horus* and four goddesses: *Imsety,* the human-headed genie of the South, protects the liver with *Isis; Hapy,* the baboon-headed genie of the North, protects the lungs with *Nephthys; Duamutef,* the jackal-headed genie of the East protects the stomach with *Neith; Qebehsenuef,* the falcon-headed genie of the West, protects the intestines with *Selkis.*

By following these operations, the deceased can become an *"Osiris,"* the god who was murdered by his brother *Seth* and brought back to life by his sister-wife *Isis,* who was helped during this ordeal by the jackal *Anubis,* inventor of mummification, and by the ibis *Thoth,* the master of "divine words." According to **Herodotus,** the most costly embalming processes meticulously reproduce the one performed on *Osiris.* It is accompanied with the reciting of many religious and magical formulae in which the priest-reader chants different passages of the ritual during the preparation of the body and the bandaging. When the mummy is ready to be lowered into the coffin, the ceremony comes to an end with the following words: *"You come alive, you come alive forever, you are here young once again, forever."* The deceased has conquered death and has gained eternal life.

Fans, walking sticks, crooks and royal batons

Walking stick bearing the image of Tutankhamun as a child (n°. 235a)

The walking stick is surmounted by a small tablet that bears a figurine representing Tutankhamun as a child. He wears a khepresh, the war crown with round motifs and his forehead is decorated with the uraeus.

Gold.
Tomb n°. 62,
Burial Chamber,
The Cairo Museum.

Pages 88-89
"The golden fan" (n°. 242)

The iconography chosen to decorate this fan (although the feathers have now disappeared) is both unique and exquisite: it recounts one of young Tutankhamun's "expeditions" during a hunt where he can be seen killing the ostriches whose feathers will then be used to make the article. This event must have impressed his entourage as it has been inscribed on the handle and the semi-circular palm.

Wood coated with a thick sheet of gold.
Tomb n°. 62,
Burial Chamber,
The Cairo Museum.

Whatever the period, figurative representations and statuary elements present characters (be they men or gods) that carry walking sticks, crooks or batons. This type of objects had appeared long before *Tutankhamun's* tomb was discovered. Thus, what surprised the archaeologists in this tomb was the great amount of them that had been placed beside the king. In fact, **Carter** imagined for an instant that he could have collected them. There were more than one hundred and thirty objects all jumbled together but all different. There were ritual objects (ceremonial batons) and functional objects (weapons, instruments for killing dangerous animals...). All were crafted in different ways: simple batons or long round-shaped batons, crooks with curved ends, walking sticks with slightly forked handles, with knobs or decorated with figurines... Some models had safety catches that stopped them from being used. There were many types of objects made in many types of materials: ebony, ivory, gold, silver, glass, bark... *"Some sticks were sculpted in the finest gold or silver, whilst other were made of undecorated polished wood or simply decorated with bark marquetry,"* explains **Carter.**

Some articles are extremely noteworthy, specially the superb walking stick (n°. 250uu) found in the **Antechamber** which bears two captives at the bottom with entwined arms and legs; one is sculpted in ebony representing a Nubian, the other sculpted in ivory, represents an Asian. Two other impressive walking sticks are nos. 235a and 235b, both long and thin, found in the **Burial Chamber** resting against the door of the first shrine. The first is made of gold, the second of silver; they are both surmounted by a tablet that holds a statuette of the king. Although he wears the royal loincloth and the blue crown with the **uraeus,** *Tutankhamun* is represented more as a plump infant than as a grown man. Between the first two golden shrines found in the **Burial Chamber**, the archaeologists found a batch of sticks wrapped in a cloth. One of these surprised **Carter** greatly, being just a reed decorated with a long gold handle (n°. 229). An inscription along the baton explains this sumptuous decoration: *"Reed picked by his Majesty's own hands."*

Fans were also found among these objects, eight examples in total: two in the **Burial Chamber,** five in the **Annexe** and one in the **Treasury.** They are usually presented with a handle of varied length, consisting of a semi-elliptic or semi-circular plate which was originally embedded with feathers. The only fan that was intact when discovered was the one found in the **Treasury** (n°. 272a); it had been stored carefully in a wooden casket and still had all its feathers, which were short and black at the base, then became long and white, opening out like a large bouquet of flowers.

The two most astounding examples were the fans found in the **Burial Chamber** between the third and fourth gilt wood shrine, one on the southern side (n°. 245) and one on the western side (n°. 242). The first is known as the "ebony fan" and is composed of a semi-circular palm covered with a thick coat of gold inlaid with obsidian and glass. The cartouches of the young king appear on the palm, protected by two vultures with outstretched wings, one of them wearing the white crown of Upper Egypt and the other the red crown of Lower Egypt. Both the vultures and the cartouches are set on the **nub,** symbol of gold.

The second fan is known as the "golden fan" and is one of the masterpieces of the tomb. It is entirely coated in gold, and stands on top of a tall rod which bears an exquisite vertical inscription. We learn that young *Tutankhamun* *"like a mountain of gold that brightens the Two-Kingdoms, alongside Harakhty,"* collected the ostrich feathers used for this fan himself *"hunting in the western desert of Heliopolis."* This campaign probably impressed his sculptors as they have depicted this image on the semi-circular palm. The front shows the process being carried out: the king rides a chariot pulled by two horses, and equipped with his bow he is preparing to kill a stricken ostrich. The back recounts His Majesty's triumphant return: *"the god incarnate, a brave hunter, with the animals caught in his prestigious battles in each foreign country, his every arrow reaches its goal like those of Bastet".* The Pharaoh also appears riding his chariot but he has not put down his bow. Two servants walk before him carrying the catch of the triumphant hunt: two ostriches whose feathers shall be used to make the fan.

87

THE TREASURY
THE DEPTHS OF THE TOMB...

From autumn 1926 to winter 1927

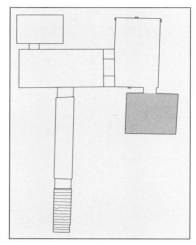

When **Carter** had the opportunity to explore the northern part of the sepulchre for the first time, on the 17th of February 1923, he immediately noticed a low door cut into the **Burial Chamber's** eastern wall. A narrow non-sealed passageway led to another room, which he called the **Treasury** given the wonders he found within. Not only were the items astounding but, most importantly, it seemed that they had not been touched since *Tutankhamun's* funeral. *"The plunderers had certainly reached this room and entered it, but they probably did not have the time to open more than two or three chests, most of the boxes were still sealed ..."*

The works began with the clearing of the **Burial Chamber**, although it took another three and a half years until the **Treasury** could finally be emptied. Meanwhile, the entrance was closed up, according to **Carter** in order to *"avoid us being distracted by all these objects."* The long-awaited day finally arrived: on the 24th of October 1926 the team lifted the wooden planks that hid the entrance to the **Treasury** and began to extract the objects with extreme care. The room was slightly bigger than the **Annexe:** it measured 15 feet 5 inches long by 12 feet 4 inches wide; and was much less cluttered with items. **Carter** catalogued seventy-six batches numbered from

261 to 336, containing approximately five hundred objects (the **Annexe** contained more than two thousand). However, there was a noticeable difference in their quality: here, each item was a gem and had a uniquely funerary function. In the first place, they removed the **naos** that was placed in front of the entrance to the room which was still resting on a sled; on top of it there was a majestic statue of the dog *Anubis* still covered by a linen cloth. The next object to be removed was the gilt wood cow-head found behind the **naos**. It was also draped in a piece of linen material, and symbolised goddess *Hathor*, protector of the Theban necropolis. The objects that were leaning against the northern wall of the room could then be removed: small-scale models of boats, pieces of chariots and fragments of chests or chests full of jewels, **shabtis** and other precious statuettes. Finally, the team moved onto the southern wall, mainly inspecting the monument that had left **Carter** dumbfounded when he saw it for the first time: the shrine-shaped chest that contained the royal Canopic jars. Along the wall, among the reproductions of boats and the boxes, they found a chest containing two mummified foetuses, the bed of *Osiris*, a model of a hayloft, various **naos** with gilt statues representing the deceased...

THE SHRINE-SHAPED CHEST CONTAINING THE CANOPIC JARS

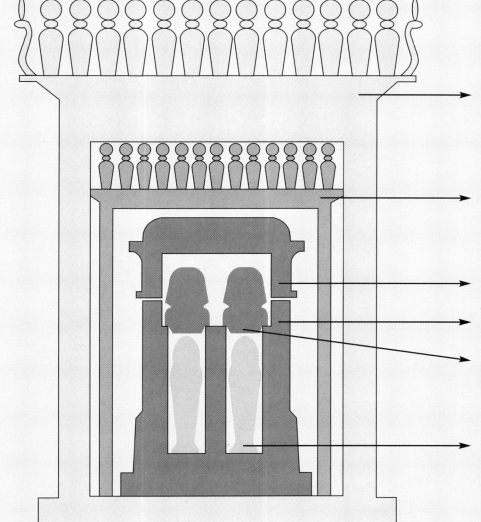

THE SHRINE-SHAPED CHEST SEEN IN SECTION

Gilt wood canopy (n° 266a) composed by four corner posts with a cornice crowned with a frieze of uraei.

Gilt wood shrine (n° 266a) surmounted by a cornice of sacred cobras. The four goddesses that protect the deceased appear on the walls, between the corner posts of the canopy: Neith at the North, Nephthys at the East, Selkis at the South and Isis at the West (the deities do not appear on the sketch).

Lid of the chest with calcite Canopic Jars (n° 266b). It was found wrapped in a linen shroud

Chest with calcite Canopic Jars (n° 266b) divided into four cylindrical compartments.

Lid of the Canopic jars (n° 266c to f). A lid bearing a human head surmounts each compartment of the chest with calcite Canopic Jars (n°. 266b). The figure is wearing a nemes decorated with the two protective deities of Egypt: Wadjit, the cobra of Lower Egypt, and Nekhbet, the vulture of Upper Egypt.

Gold coffin (n° 266g). each compartment enclosed a small gold coffin that contained the organs of the mummified king.

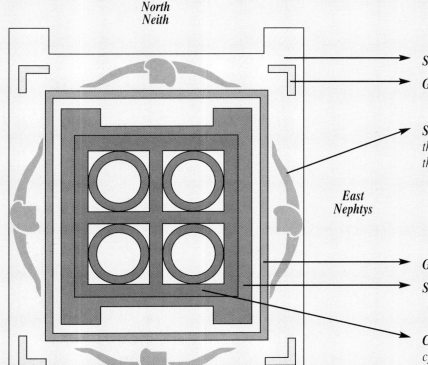

*North
Neith*

TOP VIEW OF THE SHRINE-SHAPED CHEST

Sled that supports the gilt wood canopy.

Gilt wood canopy (n° 266a) composed of four corner posts.

Statue of a goddess. The four goddesses that were to protect the deceased were depicted on the walls of the shrine, between the corner posts: Neith, Nephthys, Selkis and Isis.

*West
Isis*

*East
Nephtys*

Gilt wood shrine (n° 266a).

Sled that supports the chest with calcite Canopic Jars.

Chest with calcite Canopic Jars (n° 266b) divided into four cylindrical compartments that held the deceased's mummified internal organs. The walls are decorated with images of the Canopic protective deities (the four Sons of Horus): Duamutef (stomach), Qebehsenuef (intestines), Hapy (lungs) and Imsety (liver)

*South
Selkis*

**Canopy and shrine
with Canopic jars
(n° 266a)**

*Although the canopy and the
shrine are independent, they are
presented together forming a
whole, and have been given one
single number in Carter's
registration process. Composed
of four corner posts and a cavetto
cornice surmounted by a frieze of
uraei, the canopy protects the
shrine, which is also surmounted
by a frieze of uraei and placed
under the protection of the four
tutelary Canopic goddesses: Isis,
Nephthys, Selkis and Neith.*

Gilt wood with faience and
coloured glass inlays.
Tomb n°. 62, Treasury.
The Cairo Museum.

The shrine-shaped chest with Canopic jars

One of the first stages of the embalming ritual consists in making a small incision at flank-level through which the deceased's entrails would be extracted. Only four elements were kept, and then submitted to a particular treatment: they were mummified and placed in four urns called Canopic jars. The internal organs that were conserved were placed under the protection of the four goddesses and the *four Sons of Horus*. These genii, who are believed to be the offspring of the falcon god, were charged with ensuring the good condition of the liver, the lungs, the stomach and the intestines; both during the life of the person and in his afterlife. In Egyptian mythology they are also considered the "Lords of the cardinal points;" this function is conserved in their role as protectors of the Canopic jars, as each organ must be orientated according to its corresponding tutelary god. Thus, the rules regarding the location of these jars are very precise: *Imsety,* deity of the South, and *Isis,* watch over the liver; *Hapy,* deity of the North, and *Nephthys* watch over the lungs; *Duamutef,* deity of the East, and *Neith,* watch over the stomach; *Qebehsenuef,* deity of the West, and *Selkis,* watch over the intestines. In *Tutankhamun's* tomb the traditional rules have not been followed altogether correctly, given that on the outer shrine the two pairs of goddesses have been inverted: *Selkis* on the South and *Isis* on the West; *Neith* on the North and *Nephthys* on the East.

This shrine-shaped chest containing Canopic jars was found pushed against the wall and is considered one of the greatest masterpieces of the tomb. It is both exceptional and unique. It is composed of various elements that are interlinked with each other: a gilt wood canopy and shrine, a hollow calcite chest with four compartments closed by a lid bearing the god's image; four gold coffins containing the mummified organs.

Although they can be separated, the canopy and the shrine (n°. 266a) form a whole that rests on the same sled. Composed by four inscribed corner posts, the canopy is an open-work structure topped with a cavetto cornice surmounted by a frieze of **uraei** (thirteen cobras on each side) all inlaid with faience and coloured glass, crowned with a sun disc. Underneath this structure is the shrine, a kind of tabernacle manufactured identically to the canopy, with a cavetto cornice and frieze of cobras. Burial texts and representations are inscribed on the walls and present the Canopic protective deities. These beautiful images are ignored due to the four gilt wood statues that have been placed between the posts of the canopy. With their face turned slightly sideways and arms outstretched against the shrine in a symbol of protection, *Nephthys, Isis, Selkis* and *Neith* tenderly watch over the deceased. The long pleated robes and the proportions of the bodies of the goddesses are strongly based on Amarnian canons. A line of black kohl delicately underlines each eye and eyebrow, giving life to the godly faces.

The shrine held a calcite chest (n°. 266b), which was shrouded with a dark coloured cloth. This object, carved from a single block of white-streaked stone, replaces the four traditional Canopic jars generally used to keep the entrails. Here, each compartment has been hollowed out in the body of the chest, and a lid placed on top of each one. This cube-shaped item is surmounted by a sloped roof and decorated with a gilt wood plinth

THE PROTECTION GIVEN BY THE CANOPIC JARS

THE SOUTH	*ISIS*	*IMSETY*	protect the **liver**
	Woman crowned with the symbol that represents her name (high backed seat)	**human**-headed genie	
THE NORTH	*NEPHTYS*	*HAPY*	protect the **lungs**
	Woman crowned with the symbols that represent her name (basket and the plan of a house)	**baboon**-headed genie	
THE EAST	*NEITH*	*DUAMUTEF*	protect the **stomach**
	Woman crowned with the emblem of two bows linked together in a case	**jackal**-headed genie	
THE WEST	*SELKIS*	*QEBEHSENUEF*	protect the **intestines**
	woman crowned with the image of a scorpion or an acephalus larva	**falcon**-headed genie	

Calcite chest (nº. 266b) and Canopic jar lids (nos. 266c to f)

Enclosed in the shrine, the chest holding Canopic jars is made up of two elements: the chest proper, covered in magical texts painted black and adorned with a gilt wood plinth decorated with djed pillars and tit knots. The second element is the lid in the form of Per-wer, the primitive Southern shrine, recognisable through its single slope. The inner part is divided in four cylindrical compartments that hold the gold coffins that contain the internal organs. These compartments are sealed with elegant stoppers bearing images of Tutankhamun that are facing each other two by two.

Painted calcite and gilt wood.
Tomb nº. 62, Treasury.
The Cairo Museum.

adorned with **djed** pillars and **tit** knots and rests upon a sled with bronze handles. The four tutelary goddesses are represented on each corner: *Neith* on the south-eastern corner, *Selkis* on the north-eastern one, *Isis* on the south-western one and *Nephthys* on the north-western one. They are sculpted in bas-relief influenced by Amarnian canons: they outstretch their arms, in a symbol of protection, against the walls of the chest which are decorated with black magical inscriptions. The lid is adorned with a winged sun disc and sealed to the body of the chest by threads that are knotted around gold rings. Once the lid has been removed, it reveals four other lids (nos. 266c to f) that seal the hollows that contain the organs. The heads were made to resemble **Tutankhamun** and are placed on the lids facing each other two by two; on them the king is wearing the **nemes** and his forehead is decorated with the vulture of Upper Egypt and the cobra of Lower Egypt. His features are painted in black: his iris, the outline of his eyes and his eyebrows are adorned with a thick black streak that stretches towards his temples, the folds of the eyelids and neck are marked with a fine line. His plump

mouth is tinted red and his ears are pierced with big holes, trait of the Amarnian canon. Finally, the four gold coffins (nº. 266g) were unveiled, placed in cylindrical receptacles. When they were discovered they were wrapped in a linen shroud and covered in resin. They resemble the second royal coffin, presenting *Tutankhamun* as *Osiris*, his head wrapped in the **nemes**, with the cobra and the vulture on his forehead, and the godly false beard; his arms are crossed over his chest holding the **heka** sceptre and the flail. His body is adorned with **rishi** decoration completely inlaid with coloured glass and carnelian. The inner walls are covered with a double sheet of gold on which twenty-three lines of texts are engraved quoting the name of the deity that protects the organ contained inside the coffin. Some parts bear the sovereign's cartouches, although they had initially borne a different name, which indicates that the objects were not initially intended for Tutankhamun. The most credible hypothesis concludes these coffins, and the other objects found in the tomb, were initially meant for the mysterious **Smenkhkara**.

Jewels and ornaments

Apart from the amulets and jewels found on the mummy, the tomb also contained many other ornaments which had initially been arranged in different chests or baskets left in the various quarters. **Carter** catalogued more than two hundred items in total but, according to his estimations, the plunderers had stolen more than 60% of the jewels. Given the scarce amount of time and the narrowness of the passage covered in rubble, the plunderers had settled for the most precious and less cumbersome objects, i.e. jewels, beauty products made from rare essences and the gold or silver dinner service. The approximate evaluation of the losses was assessed through the inscriptions that quoted the exact contents of the boxes when they were placed in the tomb during the funeral. When **Carter** entered the sepulchre, he noticed that most of the seals had been broken on the caskets and the treasures they contained had been overturned. Although some items where retrieved (at the entrance of the tomb, in the entrance passageway or simply flung on the floor), others never appeared.

There are many different categories of jewels: breastplates, collars and necklaces (which were the most common by far), and also earrings, rings and bracelets. The majority of these items were found in the **Treasury**, where most of *Tutankhamun's* most precious objects had been originally stored. Some articles show clear traces of use, indicating they were worn by the king during his life; however, this is not the usual case, most of the ornaments were crafted exclusively for the funeral, as the iconography demonstrates. Although **Carter** was truly astounded by the exquisiteness of these items, some jewels proved to be more valuable and of greater quality than others: some certainly give evidence of a hasty craft, whereas many hours of work must have been needed to craft others. The same goes for the materials they are elaborated with: the rarest metals are placed next to resin or simple shells. In fact, the aspect that catches the eye, whatever the craft of the item, is the subtle display of colours: gold, silver, electrum, bronze and iron appear combined with feldspar or serpentine greens, carnelian reds, lapis lazuli or turquoise blues, calcite whites, steatite creams, amethyst violets... all brightened by the multiple shades of faience or coloured glass.

A solid gold pendant (n°. 320c) was found among the wonders discovered in the **Treasury.** The actual jewel is elegantly mounted on a gold chain, and is just 2 inches high. It is a figurine that depicts a kneeling infant who carries the royal attributes: **khepresh** war crown and **uraeus** on his head, crook and flail in his right hand. Thus, these features have led to the belief it is the representation of a sovereign, although the identity of the king it represents is still unclear given that it is unmarked. The jewel was found in very strange circumstances: it had been placed in a minuscule gilt sarcophagus, bearing the name and image of *Tutankhamun*, which was then stored in a wooden coffin that had been sealed and covered in bitumen.

Two other sarcophagi were found beside it, one inside the other; the biggest bore the names and titles of queen *Tiy*, Great Royal Wife of *Amenhotep III*. The smaller coffin bore a lock of hair wrapped in a linen cloth. Many Egyptologists have found a link between this seemingly eclectic group of items: they believe it has been conserved as a family heritage which proves that *Amenhotep III* and *Tiy* were *Tutankhamun's* parents. Yet, it is possible that the image is not of *Amenhotep III* but of the pharaoh *Tutankhamun* himself. In this case, how can the presence queen *Tiy's* name on the coffin be explained? Also fascinating are two pairs of earrings made of cloisonné gold, inlaid with multicoloured glass paste (n°. 269 and 267). The most stunning item is the earring which bears the body of a falcon surmounted by a cobalt blue duck-head as its main motif (n°. 269a-1). **Carter** also found another stunning pair which present *Tutankhamun* carved in carnelian and flanked by two **uraei**, an association which allows the proposition of a new spelling of the king's name (n°. 269a-3). They also contained various pendants which attracted the attention of the archaeologists, mainly the baboon breastplate (n°. 2671) on which two baboons, emblems of Thoth, the master of time, place their hands on the scarab Khepri, the rising sun: this scene, a type of passport to eternity, symbolises the rebirth of the king and his identification with the sun king.. The ensemble is decorated with hieroglyphic symbols invested with magical powers: the **ankh**, cross of life; the **chen**, symbol of eternity; the **was** sceptre of the gods…

THE SYMBOLS:
AMULETS, SCEPTRES AND DIVINITIES

The ankh cross
symbol of life and the breath of life

The chen symbol
of "that which the sun surrounds", i.e. the universe

The djed pillar
symbol of strength and stability

The ib heart
symbol of intelligence and conscience

The tit knot (knot of Isis)
ensures protection under every circumstance

The Hathor sistrum
symbol of music, festivities and sacred rituals

The kheper scarab
symbol of existence par excellence

The papyrus stem
symbol of fertility, fecundity and vigour

The wadjet-eye (Horus eye)
symbol of health, integrity and plenitude

The sign of the Nub gold
symbol of the unalterable nature of the divine body

 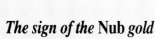

The heka sceptre (crook)
generally held by Osiris and the Pharaoh

The nekhakha flagellum (flail)
generally held by *Osiris* and the Pharaoh

The was sceptre (dog-headed baton)
held by gods and goddesses

The double feather (arrow) surmounted by an emblem
symbol of the East and the countries within

The feather on a mast
symbol of the West and the countries

The sema-tawi
symbol of the union between the two kingdoms of Egypt

 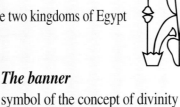

The banner
symbol of the concept of divinity

The cartouche
symbol of the universal reign of the Pharaoh

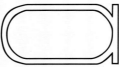 

The Maat feather
symbol of truth and justice

The obelisk
symbol of a ray of sun that evokes the veneration of the sun

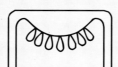 

Amun
man crowned with an inverted ortarboard with two feathers

Anubis
man with a jackal head or represented as a jackal

Apophis
giant evil serpent

Aten
sun disc with rays ending in outstretched hands

Bes
bearded dwarf with twisted legs and jovial features

Hathor
cow or cow-headed woman with horns that surround the sun disc

Harakhty
falcon crowned with the sun disc

Horus
falcon wearing with the crown of Upper and Lower Egypt (pschent)

Isis
woman crowned with a high backed seat (symbol of Isis)

Khepri
scarab or winged scarab

Maat
woman crowned with an ostrich feather

Neith
woman crowned with two bows that are joined together in their case (symbol of Neith)

Nekhbet
vulture wearing the white crown of the South

Nephtys
woman crowned with a basket and the plan of a house

Osiris
man wearing the crown of the South with two feathers (atef crown)

 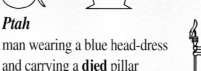

Wadjit
cobra wearing with the red crown of Lower Egypt

Ptah
man wearing a blue head-dress and carrying a **djed** pillar

Ra
man crowned with the sun disc or the sun disc

Selkis
scorpion or woman crowned with a scorpion skin

Seth
mythical animal or man with the head of said animal

Thoth
ibis or baboon or man with the head of an ibis or baboon

Teweret
woman with a hybrid body or a hybrid hippopotamus

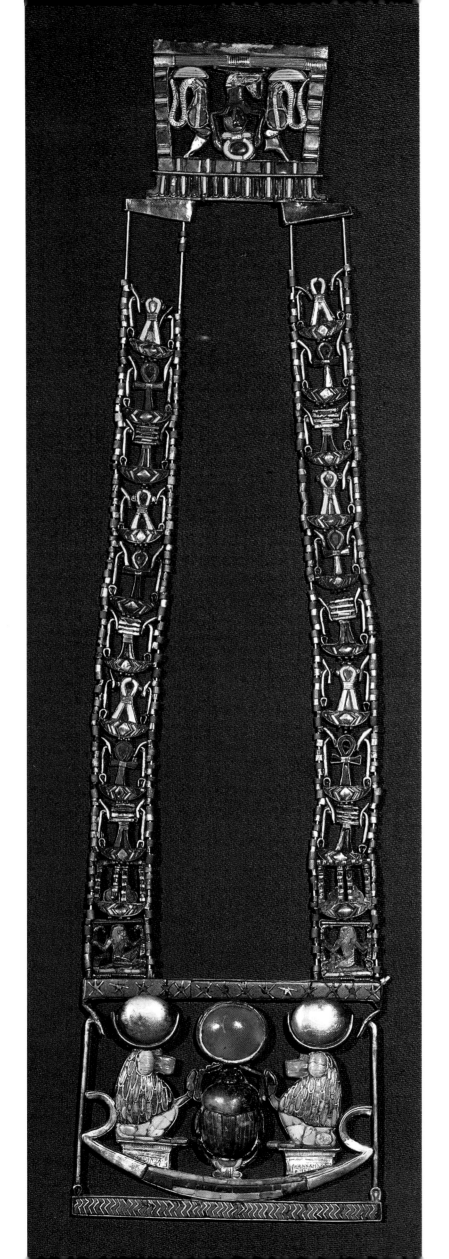

103

Divine or royal statues

The searches carried out in the **Valley of the Kings** since the beginning of the Twentieth Century had brought Egyptologists to revail the existence of these statues, both through the representations that appeared on the walls of certain tombs, mainly that of *Sety II* , and the actual discovery of some statues, found in non-archaeological contexts. *Tutankhamun's* sepulchre offered a great variety of this type of images and contributed to clarifying the ritual meaning of the room chosen to deposit these items.

The tomb contained a batch of thirty-five statues representing a variety of characters: the king (seven items), different deities of the Egyptian pantheon (twenty-eight items) two of which were found in the **Antechamber**, one in the **Burial Chamber** and thirty-two in the **Treasury**. The latter were found stored in twenty-two small wooden shrines covered in bitumen and sealed during the funeral. The plunderers had only profaned one of these **naos**, all the others still bore intact seals most probably because time was pressing against the robbers when they reached this section.

All the statues were draped in long linen cloths that covered their whole body revealing only the head. The back of the cloths bore inscriptions stating that they had been made in **Akhetaten**, the royal city of *Amenhotep IV*. Some indicated the year when they were woven: the third year of *Akhenaten's* reign. It seems none of them were initially woven for the young king but had instead been created for his predecessor before he broke off relations with the clergy of *Amun*. As they had not been used for the funeral of the heretic pharaoh, they had been set aside, placed in the stock room and recovered for *Tutankhamun's* funeral. Could this also be the case of the actual statues, which all present a heavy influence of the Amarna period? Egyptologists have not yet agreed on an answer: some believe they are all part of a batch conceived originally for *Akhenaten* and crafted at the beginning of his reign, whilst for others these traits followed the revival of **Amarna**, used on statues that date from the first years of *Tutankhamun's* reign. *"They are both spontaneous and natural,"* says **Carter**, *"the emotion that brings them to life goes beyond pure convention, they link force and charm, intimately joining the human and the divine."*

Most of the items are made of wood, coated with stucco and completely gilt; only the inlaid eyes and the eyebrows stand out. Whether they represent royal or divine figures, the statues are presented standing up, usually walking, wearing sandals and carrying complements crafted in gilt copper (sceptres, batons and walking sticks). They are placed on a bitumen-coated base, onto which the names of the depicted pharaoh and god have been inscribed. They present a great variety of attitudes, especially those that represent *Tutankhamun:* the sovereign walking, small figurines of the mummified king sitting on the head of goddess *Menkeret*, effigies representing the young king as *Horus* using a harpoon to execute *Seth's* hippopotamus, representations showing the pharaoh upon the back of a leopard. Some items have nothing in common with these gilt wood models, especially the astounding statues of *Tutankhamun* depicted as the god *Ihy* (nos. 275a and 289c). These are carved from sycamore wood and totally covered in bitumen, resembling the fragments that had been found previously in the **Valley of the Kings**. Whatever the real magic powers of these statues were, it has been proven that their colour is not important, given that black and gold are the two symbols of regeneration and rebirth.

Ihy, a child god believed to be the son of *Hathor* and *Horus,* adopts the iconography reserved exclusively for god-sons or young children: he is naked, his head still bears the sidelock of youth, a braided lock of hair that was worn on the right side of the scalp falling past the right shoulder. The eyes and eyebrows are underlined with a thick stroke of gold paint that stretches out towards the temples. He is depicted in a walking position, the left leg placed slightly before the right one, holding a sistrum in his right hand; this instrument is the trait of *Hathor, "goddess of music and dance."* Thus the pharaoh is obviously depicted as the son of *Hathor.* It is believed that *Ihy* is *"the embryo of the being devoid of his past forms."* When the figure is black this represents that he is still in the kingdom of darkness, where he must protect himself from all those who wish to stop him developing. However, if he should encounter any obstacles, he must shake his sistrum and the goddess will appear, helping him to reach the end. *Ihy* represents the king in a new way: he comes to life in the realm of the gods.

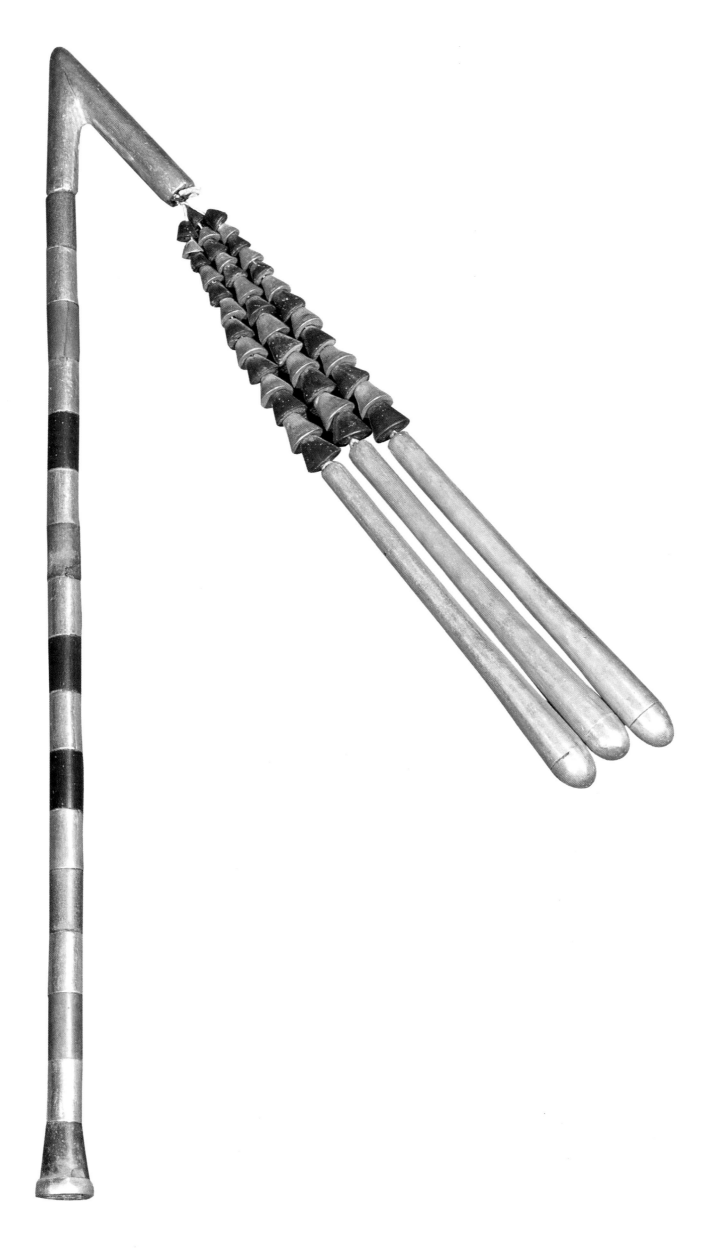

Sceptres

The **Treasury** enclosed two pairs of sceptres: both were composed of a **heka** crook (n°. 269d and n°. 269h) and a **nekhakha** flail (n°. 269f and n°. 269e), both insignia of royalty. In fact, these complements belong to none other than *Osiris,* ruler of the dead. One may wonder what links the pharaoh to *Osiris* given that their symbols are identical. In order to understand this assimilation, one must refer to the Osirian legend and a gaze must be cast towards the time when men and gods walked the earth. It is believed that, from father to son, the line of succession was from *Ra* to *Shu* to *Geb* and finally to *Osiris.* The latter was murdered by his brother Seth and brought back to life with the care of Isis, *Anubis* and *Thoth* who, after collecting the different parts of the body of the god which had been scattered all over the country, carried out the first mummification process, allowing *Osiris* to rule the Netherworld. However, the murder of the god gave way to a problem in the succession to the Egyptian throne, thus a battle was fought between the two heirs: *Horus,* the son of *Osiris* and *Isis,* and *Seth.* After years of trials, the verdict favoured Horus who officially inherited the earthly throne. Therefore, the Pharaoh, direct successor of Horus is believed to be his incarnation on earth: he is the legitimate descendant of the line of god-kings. According to this, is it quite logical that the emblems carried by the lords of royalty, be they earthly or heavenly, should be passed down through the generations. This is the case of the crook and flail, insignia of *Osiris,* the god who died and was born anew.

The two pairs of sceptres found in the **Treasury** are quite similar. The handles are made of thick tubular beads made of blue glass or metallic gold-plated elements. The whole piece is mounted on a rod made of a copper alloy, with a gilt tip which is inscribed. The crook from the first set (n°. 269d) bears *Tutankhamun's* coronation name in a cartouche: *"Nebkheperura"*, surrounded by two erect uraei. The flail (n°. 269f) is inscribed with two cartouches side by side bearing the king's coronation name and also the name of the sun disc: *"Living Aten"*. Undoubtedly, this pair was made for the young king's coronation, when he was only nine years old and the worship of *Aten* had not yet been completely eradicated

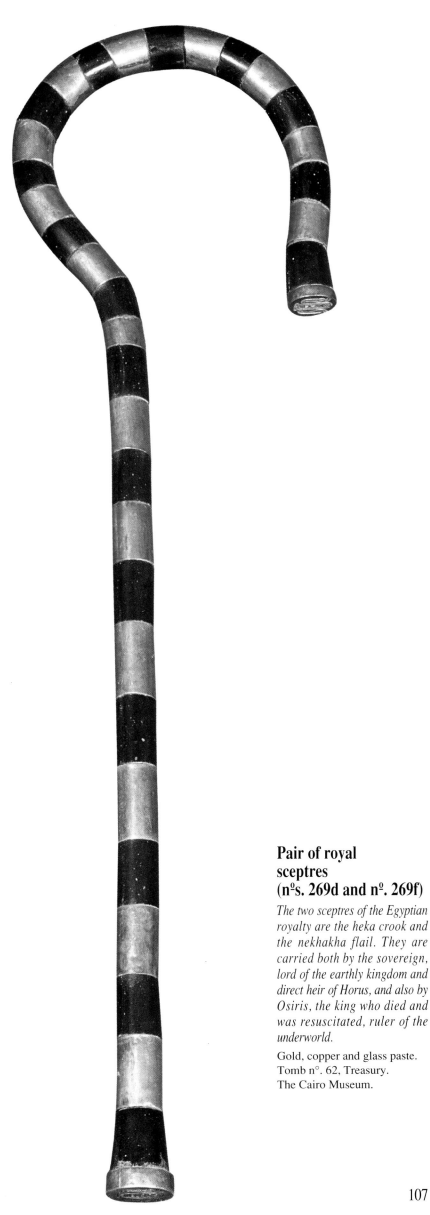

Pair of royal sceptres (n°s. 269d and n°. 269f)

The two sceptres of the Egyptian royalty are the heka crook and the nekhakha flail. They are carried both by the sovereign, lord of the earthly kingdom and direct heir of Horus, and also by Osiris, the king who died and was resuscitated, ruler of the underworld.

Gold, copper and glass paste.
Tomb n°. 62, Treasury.
The Cairo Museum.

The wooden shabti of Tutankhamun

**The wooden shabti
of Tutankhamun
(n° 331a)**

*This statuette represents the
mummified sovereign represented
as Osiris lying on a low bier. Two
birds protect him: the human-
headed bird, symbol of the ba, i.e.
the king's spirit, and a falcon-
headed bird that represents
the god Horus. This wooden
shabti was an offering made by
Maya, Treasury Official, for
Tutankhamun's funeral.*

Painted wood.
Tomb n°. 62, Treasury.
The Cairo Museum.

This figurine (n°. 331a) was found in the **Treasury** near the boxes that contained the shabtis and the divine statues. It was inside a sarcophagus made of wood that had been blackened with bitumen. It has been crafted out of a single block of wood (most probably cedar-wood), with undulated striations which the sculptor has used in a most admirable way. The material is so pure that just a few traces of paint have been needed to mark the essential details. The statue represents a mummified *Tutankhamun,* wearing a **nemes** head-cloth and a **uraeus** adorning his forehead. On either side of the body, two birds extend a protective wing over the king's chest. The **ba,** representing the deceased's spirit, is depicted on the left, symbolised with a human-headed bird: this is *Osiris,* symbol of that which belongs to the past. Depicted on the right is a falcon-headed bird that embodies the regeneration of the pharaoh after his long journey in the underworld: this is *Horus,* symbol of that which belongs to the future. His body is decorated with strips of inscriptions –one vertical and four horizontal–

that place the pharaoh under the protection of the burial deities: they invoke *Osiris, Horus* and *Anubis,* alongside the four *Sons of Horus,* the guardians of the internal organs. The text that appears at *Tutankhamun's* feet appeals to Nut: *"Mother Nut, spread yourself over me, place me among the imperishable stars which are in you."*

The bier the mummy lies upon is engraved with an inscription that quotes that the figurine was but a burial present offered to the king by **Maya,** *"useful servant to his master, who searches for good and does what he should do, who executes things perfectly for his master in the Sublime Place, Head of all the works in the Place of Truth, on the Western bank, beloved by his master and carries out the orders he receives, not tolerating failure, whose face never lies, who performs everything with a loving heart, doing the useful things his master loves."* This high official, one of the people who was closest to the young sovereign was most probably he who saved *Tutankhamun's* tomb from robberies on two occasions.

Cosmetic items

The tomb contained a series of cosmetic items; some had obviously been used by the king during his life, others had been manufactured for his life in the Netherworld. They were mostly found in the **Treasury, Antechamber** and **Annexe,** placed inside chests: perfume vases, ointment pots, make-up spoons, tubes of kohl, mirrors and cases, ewers, razor blades and linen were discovered.

There are three noteworthy objects in the collection, specially the golden ointment pot (nº. 240bis). It is composed by two small royal cartouche-shaped boxes, welded together and surmounted by ostrich feathers surrounding the sun disc; the whole is inlaid with coloured glass and semi-precious stones. The main interest this item presents is the iconography chosen to decorate the main sides of the two compartments which bear a rare iconography of the pharaoh's prenomen, *"Nebkheperura", "Supreme manifestation of Ra."* In this case *"kheperu"* usually composed of *kheper,* the scarab, and *u,* three strokes that denote the plural form, is

replaced by an image that depicts the sovereign crouching and crowned with a **khepresh** on one side and a sidelock of youth on the other. The different range of colours chosen to tinge *Tutankhamun's* skin reflects the different transformations: childhood, adulthood, death and rebirth.

Two beautiful mirror cases were found in the **Treasury,** made of gilt wood and were given catalogue numbers 269b and 271c-d. The first is crafted in the shape of a cross of life, a subtle play on words in hieroglyphic language given that *ankh* means "life" and also "mirror.." The second case represents *Heh,* god of Eternity, who is depicted with his usual iconography: kneeling he holds palm-tree leaves over a *chen* symbol and the sign of the frog. A big sun disc (slightly oval-shaped) appears over his head surrounded by the royal cartouches, destined to protect the mirror itself. **Carter** never found the mirrors that belonged to these cases: they were probably made of gold, silver or bronze and had been stolen by the plunderers.

THE ANNEXE
THE DREAM IS ACCOMPLISHED...

From autumn 1927 to spring 1928

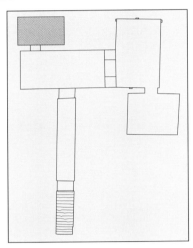

The **Annexe** was the last room **Carter** and his team cleared. The works commenced on the 30th of October 1927, and before they had even started to attempt clearing the room, the archaeologists already knew how ample this task would be as they has entered the room during the first exploration of the tomb, on the 27th of November 1923. Thus, astounded by the great pile of objects, **Carter** could not keep from thinking that *"when the moment came for clearing this chamber, it would be extremely different to decide where to begin."* The **Annexe** had a north-south orientation and was the smallest room in the tomb, measuring only 14 feet 2 inches long by 8 feet 5 inches wide. However, it was the most crammed and cluttered room: it held two hundred and eighty-four batches, catalogued from numbers 337 to 620, containing more than two thousand objects composing more than half of the material found in the whole sepulchre.

At first, the excavators were surprised at the chaos that reigned in the **Annexe**; however, after reconstructing the story of the different robberies of the tomb, they realised that the room was still in the state that the plunderers had left it. The necropolis officials had attempted to tidy the other three rooms before reclosing them. This was a different case; not only had they ignored

everything but they had also left the doorway that separated the **Annexe** from the **Antechamber** unsealed. Was this because they did not have enough time, had they been careless, or had they simply forgotten it? Whatever the case, and despite the difficult situation, the clearing works had to be carried out. The question was how to do it? Everything had been overturned, thrown onto the floor or stacked, sometimes in piles of almost 7 feet high. The archaeologists devised a system of props and supports to avoid objects crashing to the ground and started clearing the chamber from south to north. Sometimes they swung on ropes to attain certain objects that were out of reach or extremely delicate. The clearing process was obviously long and, at times, tiresome. **Carter** was perplexed at the diversity of the material stored in the **Annexe**: he had a hard time trying to determine the primary function of the eclectic range of items from this chamber. He concluded that the chamber had been conceived to store ointments and provisions: he had found alabaster oil-vases, wine jars and food baskets. Nonetheless, the room also contained military items, **shabtis**, burial furniture, crooks, walking sticks and games, which would all have undoubtedly been placed in the **Antechamber** or the **Treasury** if the sepulchre had been more spacious

Ointment vase (n°. 578)

This boat shaped receptacle has a decorated central deckhouse, and two tips finishing in ibex heads with real horns. It is the best-crafted ointment vase found among the whole of Tutankhamun's treasures. The young girl who is kneeling at the front of the boat is believed to be one of the royal princesses, Ankhesenamun's sister.

Calcite with gold and painted ornaments.
Tomb n°. 62, Annexe.
The Cairo Museum.

Vases and receptacles

A great number of these objects were found in the sepulchre and can be divided into four different categories according to the material they are made of: stone, metal, glass and faience, ceramic. For **Carter** the stone vases were the most interesting as they *"aroused amazement, mixed with curiosity and admiration."* Most of them are made of calcite, then gilt, painted or inlaid with semi-precious stones and fragments of coloured glass, although some rare examples made in limestone and serpentine were also found. They were conceived to contain cosmetic products, oils and perfumes. Almost eighty different models were found mainly in the **Antechamber** and the **Annexe** in many different forms: jars, pots, urns, vases, amphorae or extremely well crafted receptacles, goblets, seals, cups, bowls and ewers. **Carter** noted two anomalies in the composition of this eclectic batch which led him to believe certain items had not been manufactured for *Tutankhamun* but had been taken from the stock of a royal store-room: various vases bore the cartouches of *Thutmose III*, of *Amenhotep III*, of queen *Tiy*, of the young king's wife, *Ankhesenamun*, or of *Djehutymose*, one of **Maya's** assistants (Director of all the works in the **Place of Truth**), whilst others presented traces of having been broken and repaired in ancient times.

There are various noteworthy items among this batch of receptacles with a range of capacities between 2.75 and 14 litres. Firstly, the two extraordinary ointment vases found in the **Annexe**. The first (n°. 578) is shaped as a ceremonial baton placed on a high base and mounted on a small chest; the whole is decorated with a mosaic of lotus flowers and geometric elements. Both ends of the boat are decorated with ibex heads, with real horns and decorated with a gold plated necklace; the centrepiece is composed of a rectangular cabin that contained the perfumes. It is sheltered by a canopy that is held up by four pillars both (painted and gilt) and crowned with a double capital with organic motifs. Two naked women appear on either side, one kneeling at the front of the boat, the other standing up at the back: the first is young and holds a lotus flower to her chest, whilst the second, who is older and seems to be a midget, holds a pole with which she guides the boat. The young kneeling princess is thought to be one of *Ankhesenamun's* sisters.

The other vase found in the **Annexe** (n°. 579) is totally different in its craft. It is shaped like a lion fiercely standing upon its back legs, the front right leg is lifted up and the left leg rests on a sign of protection bearing the **tit** knot, symbol of the goddess *Isis*. The animal is standing upon a stool which bears a geometric decoration and wears a complicated crown: a type of floral composition with an alternation of rosettes, lotus petals and papyrus stems. His great open mouth reveals eight ivory fangs and a long tongue that has been tainted red. His torso bears the cartouches of the king and the queen. Specialists have various opinions regarding the divinity that the lion represents: it could be *Bes*, the domestic protector, or *Mahe*, a divine character associated with *Nefertum*, son of *Ptah* and *Sekhmet*. This warrior god, represented as a lion *"with a terrible glare"* is the *"lord of carnage"* who is able to fight *Osiris'* enemies.

The **Burial Chamber** contained extremely well-crafted objects, especially a **sema-tawi** perfume vase (n°. 210). It has been carved out of two blocks of calcite, one used for the base and the other for the actual receptacle; the whole piece stands out given its well-balanced proportions and an almost ethereal elegance. The openwork decoration that appears on the white veiny stone resembles the **sema-tawi**, symbolised by two emblematic plants (the lotus of Upper Egypt and the papyrus of Lower Egypt). They are tied around a trachea by two *Hapy* gods, the genie of the Nile who personifies the flood and ensures fertility of the cultivated land and an abundant harvest. A vulture with outstretched wings appears at the top of the composition, whilst two gilt **uraei** appear on either side: one wearing the white crown of the South and the other the red crown of the North.

The last noteworthy stone receptacle is the cup (n°. 14) found in the entrance to the **Antechamber**. This *"chalice for the immortality of the benefactor of Thebes"* is cut in the shape of a white lotus that emerges from the water. On either side, various flower buds with the god *Heh* (symbol of eternity) grow from three stems. The text that is inscribed along the top part of the cup expresses a wish: *"You who love Thebes, may your ka live for millions of years, seated, with your face turned towards the northern wind and your eyes full of joy."*

The metallic items are distinguishable due to their great scarcity: only three items were discovered in the whole tomb, all found in the **Annexe**. Two are minuscule receptacles (nos. 390 and 620:37), barely an inch high, one gold and the other silver; the third item is an extremely well-crafted vase (n°. 469). The latter is chased in chiselled metal, in the shape of a pomegranate, a fruit that was introduced into Egypt after the victories of *Thutmose III* in Asia. The neck is decorated with motifs of lotus flowers and leaves, and two cornflowers decorate the body. *Tutankhamun's* tomb most probably contained many other metallic vases which must have been stolen by the plunderers, given their value.

The following items are crafted in glass and faience, both very widespread materials during the 18th Dynasty. Strangely enough, the tomb only contained three glass receptacles, according to **Carter** *"curiously, the glass had also been stolen."* This obviously occurred because the material was then quite precious and also recyclable: a dream target for any tomb plunderer. Two cups and a flask were found packed haphazardly in the cedar-wood casket with sliding poles (n°. 32). They were no taller than 2 or 3 inches high but gleamed in dark blue or translucent white. It is a different case for the faience items, as a great number of objects were found both in the **Annexe** and the **Antechamber**: sixty-seven objects in all. Items such as ewers, pots, cups, dishes, jars, globe-shaped receptacles, **nemset** vases or hes vases.

The last objects are those made of pottery which attracted the attention of neither **Carter** nor his team given the value and rarity of the other items found in the tomb. The articles are interesting nonetheless. They discovered around sixty receptacles: cups, saucers, plates, bowls and jars (which composed 80 % of the find). Terracotta objects were made in three designs: unmarked and undecorated, decorated with painted blue strips or bearing an ink inscription quoting their contents (beverage or food). The analysis of these inscriptions written in hieratic (a language used for civil acts), indicates that thirty of the fifty jars found in the sepulchre had been used to store wine; all were found in the Annexe. Each jar indicates the vintage year, the type of beverage (wine, sweet wine or pomegranate wine, fine or very fine quality), the vineyard (68 % of the production was from Aten's vineyards, 27 % from Tutankhamun's vineyards and 5 % from Amun's vineyards) and the prenomen of the winegrower.

Tools

These functional and ritual tools found in the tomb compose an extremely interesting batch given that some of them had only been seen before in representations on the walls of civil sepulchres (most importantly tomb n°. 100 belonging to **Rekhmira**, n°. 217 belonging to **Ipuy** or n°. 181 belonging to **Nebamun** and **Ipuki**). The range of objects consists of small-scale models or full-scale objects which had been placed in all quarters of the tomb. Most probably they had originally been stored in boxes. However, **Carter** found many of them strewn on the floor where the plunderers had left them carelessly when they had inspected the chests. Sometimes only the handles were left, the blades must have been made of gold, or at least made of a valuable metal, and the robbers must have pulled them from the handles wishing only to take precious items with them.

Objects found among the selection which can be divided into four categories: artisan tools including different types of knives, blades, scissors, mallets, pestles and sharpening stones; farming tools such as hoes, adzes, sickles, hatchets and grindstones; measuring instruments such as rulers graded in Egyptian cubits; lighting systems such as lamps, torches and items that could produce fire. The objects were made in a diversity of materials: wood, faience, flint, limestone, calcite, bronze, sandstone, gold, electrum, silver, iron, plain bricks, reeds... the most beautiful items have inlaid or inscribed decorations. Sticks, batons or ingots were made out of raw materials such as malachite, tin, chalk, galena, ochre and other pigments, resin, incense, orpiment... These were used by artisans and for pharmaceutical and cosmetic purposes.

Without a doubt, the most interesting object of all these instruments is the "lighter" (n°. 585aa) found in a chest in the **Annexe**. It was an object that produced fire and was composed of two elements: along the sides, a rectangular friction strip which was pierced with twelve holes containing resin and with gashes that allowed for the spark to spread to the tinder. The "lighter" had a cap on the top end and was linked to a bow. **Carter** explained that *"the rotation was achieved by pulling the bow from front to back; beforehand, the strip had been wrapped around the handle of the lighter to which the match was affixed."* Compared to other models used in Egypt, this is one of the most efficient mediums with which to light a fire.

Headrests

In Egypt, beds were usually equipped with headrests which were made of wood, ivory, glass paste or stone. In most cases they all present the same aspect: a base that gives them stability, a vertical support, decorated or non-decorated, and a half-moon shaped part on top of which a small linen cushion was placed to rest the head. Sometimes they are decorated with the images of popular deities, specially *Bes* and *Teweret,* who both protect the sleeper from evil sprits and genii whilst he or she sleeps. Although they are used during the life of the person, they have an essential role in the underworld.

Chapter CLXVI of the **"Book of the Dead"**, titled *"The pillow of the deceased"* quotes the functions of this object: *"You who are sick and prostrate, your body is exhausted: your raised head looks towards the Horizon, and slowly you sit up. Now, thanks to the kind deeds that the gods promised you, you can overcome the obstacles. Here is Ptah knocking down your enemies, obeying the decree of the judgement. You are Horus, son of Hathor, Nesert, Nesertet! Your head will be restored after the massacres. You must know your head will be saved! It will not be stolen for eternity."* Many examples were found in ***Tutankhamun's*** tomb, most of them in the **Annexe.**

The most magnificent object (n°. 403c) is a unique item, sculpted from two blocks of ivory which are held together by a mortice and tenon joint and two gold nails. The support represents one of the great cosmogonic divinities: *Shu,* the god of the air. He is kneeling and holds the curve of headrest as he holds *Nut,* the heavens, in the **Heliopolis** myth from which he originates. Two recumbent lions appear on the base with their back to the divinity: they are the guardians of the doors to the horizon; one watches over the East and the other over the West.

Three other headrests were found in the same chest, and are all equally remarkable: one made of lapis lazuli blue glass paste (n°. 403a) one made of dark blue faience (403b), composed of two assembled parts, the join hidden by a gilt strip; the last one was made of ivory and painted dark green, light brown and black (n°. 403d), it resembles a folding chair with legs ending in heads of ducks and ends decorated with the image of Bes, the domestic protector.

Beadhead with the image of the god Shu (n°. 403c)

This headrest is the most interesting of those found in the sepulchre. It represents Shu, the god of the air, holding Nut, the heavens. On either side of him there are two lions: they are the guardians of the horizon, one facing the East and the other the West.

Ivory and gold.
Tomb n°. 62, Annexe.
The Cairo Museum.

Writing material and musical instruments

Exquisite scribe's equipment was discovered in *Tutankhamun's* tomb, most of the objects having been stored in the **Annexe,** although some were found in the **Treasury.** They catalogued fourteen palettes, all rectangular slides with small holes in the end to hold coloured inks. All had hollow centres which stored the rushes, quills or reed brushes with a sharp end that allowed the scribe to write or draw. The palettes were usually made of wood; however, in the young king's tomb the various models, both functional and ceremonial, were made of glass, gold or silver-plated wood, ivory inlaid with precious metals. This material was complemented with a rush case made of gilt wood with incrustations, two ink goblets carved from horns, four limestone drawing palettes, a papyrus burnisher made of ivory and gold, a sandstone scraper that was used as a "rubber", a ceramic pot of paint and an assortment of colours (black, white, yellow, red and blue), some stored in shells, others in tablets or blocks.

The reasons why this material was buried alongside the Pharaoh are still uncertain, given that during his life he was not a scribe. A preliminary answer can be gained from the **"Pyramid Texts"** from the Old Kingdom, a series of formulae that guarantee the passage of the soul to the netherworld, the resurrection of the deceased and his life with the blessed. One of the passages explains that for his voyage the sovereign was called to become the scribe of *Ra,* the sun. The **"Book of the Dead"**, that was written in more recent times, gives another explanation: chapter XCIV refers to writing material, and the illustration depicts a palette and a goblet either being held by the deceased or placed on a table. The picture is accompanied by a text that announces the use of these objects: it was believed that, if the deceased held them he or she would from then on know the *"writings of the god Thoth"* which would allow the learning of the magical formulae necessary to succeed in the underworld. Palette n°. 262 bearing the name of Martinet, daughter of *Akhenaten* and wife of the symbolic *Smenkhkara* was left between the legs of a great black *Anubis* jackal in *Tutankhamun's* **Treasury.** Placed in this particular location, it became one of the instruments the soul needed to make its journey to the netherworld, as *Anubis* was the god who helped the deceased reach daylight once again.

In opposition to the abundance of writing material that was discovered in the tomb, the musical instruments stand out because of their scarcity: a trumpet was found in the **Burial Chamber**, a pair of clappers in the Annexe and two sistra and a trumpet in the Antechamber. The clappers (nos. 620:13) were made of ivory and each was shaped like an arm; they had a hole on each end that held them together so they could then be used like castanets. The fore-arms bore the cartouches of *Tiy*, the Great royal Wife, and of princess **Meritaten**, her granddaughter, although the reasons for this association remain unknown. Most probably, the two sistra (n°. 75 and n°. 76) were made up as a pair and, given their use, they could have been used during *Tutankhamun's* burial ceremonies. They had a rudimentary handle made of gilt wood and a metal loop attached to it, crossed by snake-shaped bars with small square elements, that were also made of metal, which produced a sharp sound when the object was shaken.

The most interesting items from this batch are the king's trumpets, extremely rare objects, which have been tested many times, mainly by the musician **Hans Hyckman**. He noted they made a *"hoarse, powerful sound"* that resembles the sound of a *"medieval trombone or an archaic horn,"* which confirms **Plutarch's** statement saying *"the sound of these instruments resembles the call of a donkey."* They do not make up a pair: one is made of gold and silver (n°. 175), the other of gold and bronze (n°. 50gg), they are not the same height (20 and 23 inches), and they are tuned differently. They are both composed of a long tube and a bell, which has a diameter of about 3 inches, which bears a scene decorated with a repoussé design. The silver trumpet is the most exquisite, and is decorated with the three great divinities of the pantheon: *Ra-Harakhty* from **Heliopolis,** *Amun* from **Thebes** and *Ptah* from **Memphis**. Small cartouches bearing Tutankhamun's name are vertically inscribed over them. The whole object is decorated with a lotus flower design. The copper trumpet is the most simply crafted one and only bears one central image that is framed, depicting the same three gods, but here the king appears between *Ptah* and *Amun* wearing the war crown and holding the crook and the **ankh** cross.

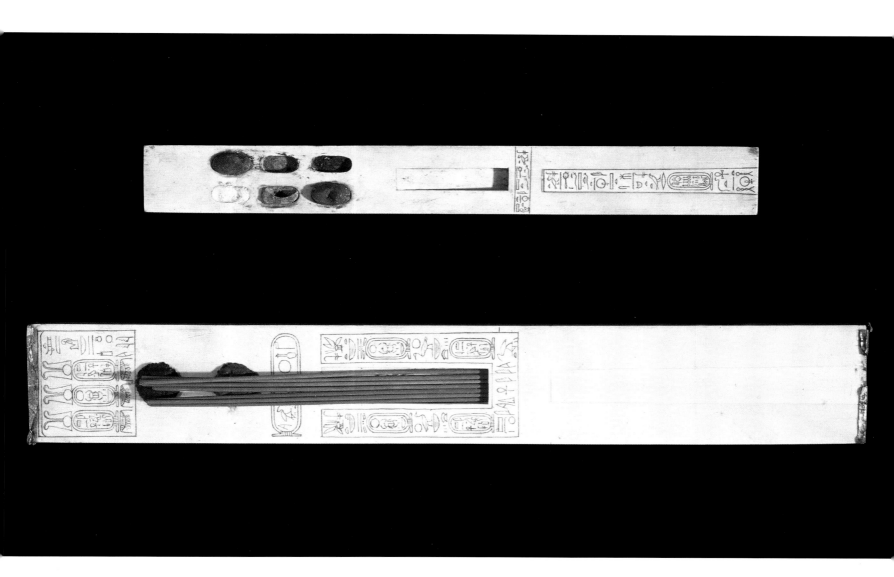

Game boards and gaming boxes

Judging by the burial representations or by the items found in various tombs, it would seem that playing games was one of the favourite Egyptian pastimes, mainly the "game of **senet**." It needs two players and is played on a board that has thirty squares in three lines of ten squares. The tokens are shared out between the players, reels for one and draughts for the other, which are then placed on the board. Then they each take turns at throwing small bones or sticks which, depending on the side they land on (black or white) allow the player to move towards the last five squares which are marked with a sign that symbolises good or bad luck. The winner is the player who clears his tokens first. At first, **senet** was a society game played to amuse the living and the dead; however, later came to be integrated into the tests that composed the judgement of the deceased. Sometimes, on funerary scenes the deceased is depicted playing against a particular adversary who is no less than a deity from the afterlife: the stake being immortality.

The **Annexe** held four board games and batches of tokens, reels, draughts, small bones and sticks (which were sometimes incomplete or unpaired). If all these objects are counted and set into groups according to their decorations or the material they are made in, there are probably two boards missing, unless the surplus consists of a spare lot of draughts that did not belong to a specific set. Whatever the case, some of the items are extremely delicate: ivory sticks with the image of African and Asian prisoners, ebony reels and draughts, ivory tokens painted with red and black stripes... The actual gaming boxes, which were initially mounted on legs that rested on a sled, bore a reversible board, one side for the "game of **senet**," the other for the "game of twenty squares," (the exact rules for this game are unknown). These tables, made in ivory or ebony, are usually inlaid with geometrical motifs or decorated with inscriptions.

Scribe palettes (n°. 271e[2] and n°. 262)

The top palette (n°. 271e[2]) bears the cartouches of Tutankhamun, "beloved of Atum, Amun-Ra and Thoth." The blocks of ink and the rushes were still inside when it was discovered. The lower palette (n°. 262) belonged to princess Meritaten, it was found between the legs of the naos that was surmounted by the image of Anubis, the jackal.

Ivory and ink.
Tomb n°. 62, Treasury.
The Cairo Museum.

Weapons

Weapons were placed in the sepulchre to allow the young king to overcome any obstacles that could endanger his voyage to the underworld. These extremely important elements were found throughout the whole vault, from the passageway to the **Treasury**, and can be grouped in various categories: sport and combat weapons, weapons with sharp blades, archery and armour.

It seems that boomerangs and snake-shaped batons were used to hunt game and fowl in marshes. Thirty-four boomerangs (either angular or with a single curve) and two batons were found in the **Annexe**. The most distinctive item of the batch is the boomerang (n°. 620:6) made out of an elephant tusk with a fine gold tip. The owner's name appears inscribed on the object: *"The good god, Lord of the Two-Lands, Nebkheperura, beloved of Ptah who is south of his wall."* Clubs (two items in gilt stucco wood), truncheons (thirteen examples made of wood, some of which have bark handles) and slings (two examples crafted from braided linen) can be grouped under the category of combat weapons. Two other objects can be added to this group: two gilt wood batons with faience tips which were found in the **Antechamber** and whose use is still unclear.

Certainly much less common were the weapons with sharp blades. Only six types were found: four swords in the **Annexe,** two of which were chased in form of gold amulets, and two daggers in the **Burial Chamber.** The swords are **khepesh** swords, often with sickle-shaped blades. They are all made of bronze, but they can be differentiated through their handles and their size: one (n°. 620:52) measures 16 inches long and its handle is crafted in dark wood, the other (n°. 582a) measures 2 inches and has a handle with inlaid wooden plates, most probably ebony wood. The daggers were found on *Tutankhamun's* mummy. The first (n°. 256dd) has a gold blade and is a wonder of the goldsmith's art. The handle is embellished with geometrical motifs and inlaid with semi-precious stones and glass, whilst the sheath, decorated with a repoussé design, represents a hunting scene in the desert with ibex and bulls attacking a cheetah, dogs and lions. The second (n°. 256k) is even more extraordinary as its blade is made of iron (a metal that was both rare and precious in the New Kingdom); it was *"still gleaming and looking like steel,"* says **Carter**. The handle is very much

the same as that of the first dagger; however, they can be differentiated by the rock crystal knob that decorates the pommel of the second. The sheath is made of gold, and chased with a **rishi** decoration with feathers on one side and a palmette and rope motif on the other.

The **Annexe** held a leather shield, a thick sleeveless corselet, and eight shields. The first four, varying in height between 34 and 35 inches, are ceremonial items that were undoubtedly used during official acts. The frame was rectangular at the base and rounded at the top, it was carved in gilt stucco wood making up a wooden panel with openwork decorations on which the pharaoh is depicted in different attitudes. The most beautiful example (n°. 379a) presents *Tutankhamun* as a human-headed sphinx trampling two African enemies with black skin. The king is wearing the striped **nemes,** the **uraeus** and the double crown of Egypt; he is protected by the falcon Horus who hovers above his head. In another remarkable item (n°. 379b) he is depicted not as a warrior but as a hunter, killing a lion with a **khepesh** sword held in his right hand. The other four shields are smaller than these (29 inches high) and less elaborate. According to **Carter**, these were functional objects, hence their less solid constitution, and consisted of a protective panel carved in gilt stucco wood which bore the cartouches of the sovereign.

The archery collection consisted of arrows, bows and quivers. The amount of items was incredible. There were one hundred and twenty seven arrows, twenty-one of which were made entirely of wood, whilst the rest were made of composite materials: bronze point, reed shaft, wooden fletching, and a point made of glass, stone, ivory, bone, wood, bronze... Fourteen ordinary bows were also catalogued, made of wood with metal handle and tips; thirty-six composite bows were also found, all noteworthy given their range. These weapons, all imported by the Hyksos invaders, are shaped like an inverted 3 and most of them have a body made of ash or elm wood, covered in bronze and sheathed in bark. One of the items in this batch is extremely noteworthy: a 4 feet 4 inches long bow (n°. 48h) called the "Bow of Honour", it is covered in a gold grain. There were four quivers made of cloth or painted wood, one of which (found in the **Treasury** (n 335), is decorated with faience, bark and gold elements.

Nourishment

Given that the funerary beliefs recounted how the deceased would come to life again in the netherworld, the deceased would obviously have to feed on something in this new existence; hence the stores of food offerings, which in certain cases were quite large. Whatever the sepulchre, the condition of the person buried within and the era, the problem of nourishment is so common that it can be thought of as an unhealthy fear of "famine." One must note that, according to tradition, *Tutankhamun's* tomb held incredible amounts of nourishment, contained in jars, baskets and boxes.

These reserves had originally been stored in the **Annexe**, but Carter found food and grain scattered over the floor throughout the whole tomb or hastily stored in the **Antechamber.** This disruption was probably caused by the two consecutive robberies. The baskets were extremely well-crafted, in many different shapes and sizes; made of leaves of date-palm trees which had been finely braided and sometimes decorated with coloured fibres which adorned the body and the lid. The boxes were more rudimentary and had all been constructed following the same pattern: they consisted of two elements which fit one on top of the other, forming an elliptical shape, and are made of mediocre quality wood, painted white on the outside and covered in black resin on the inside. *Tutankhamun's* sepulchre held sixteen baskets in the **Annexe** and forty-eight boxes in the **Antechamber**, not counting the items that were not found after the robberies and those that were scattered here and there. In some cases, mainly on boxes, an inscription indicates the nature of the food stored within. Yet, in 70% of the cases the indication is false; the reason for this is unknown, although some believe the boxes were obviously inscribed beforehand, and then during the funeral, the stated food could not be obtained.

The variety of the nourishment that was stored is amazing: different types of cakes, with or without fruits, and bread, used either for beer or to be eaten on its own, and an enormous quantity of grains, mainly barley and spelt wheat. Fruits and vegetables are represented with baskets of peas, chickpeas, onions, lentils, dates with no stones, dum-palm nuts, dry raisins, figs, almonds and watermelon seeds. The meat was mainly beef and the poultry, mainly goose

Boats

The small scale models of boats, barques, gondolas, vessels or ships that were discovered in the tomb had different functions: during the sovereign's journey to the netherworld, they allowed the deceased to sail eternally in the wake of *Ra*, the sun god; also to reach *Osiris'* kingdom, specially the Fields of Iaru, which were surrounded by dangerous waters, without having to pay tribute to the divine "ferrymen." They also allowed a pilgrimage to Abydos, *Osiris'* sacred village, and ensured the journey back; they were used to hunt the hippopotamus and the waterfowl from the marshes in the underworld, young *Horus'* mythical pastime. *Tutankhamun* had been buried with thirty-five more or less sophisticated boats which should answer all his desires; eighteen models were

FUNERARY BOATS

		Treasury	Annexe
A	Sun boats: the prow was decorated with a lotus flower turned upwards and a serrated stern; two steering-oars on the stern; a gilt throne in the centre.	4	
B	Lunar boats: prow and stern decorated with a lotus flower that is turned inwards.	2	
C	Light reed boats: flat prow and sterns.	1	1
D	Boats for fishing, transporting merchandise and navigating: serrated stern; one steering-oar; a square sail; simple decoration.		12
E	Boats for fishing, transporting merchandise and navigating: same as D but with a cabin with a game board in the centre.	1	1
F	Boats for fishing, transporting merchandise and navigating: same as D but with a cabin with a game board in the centre and a kiosk on the stern.		2
G	Boat for sailing the river: prominent prow and stern; two steering-oars; a cabin with a game board and a flat roof in the centre; with a kiosk on the stern and the prow.	7	
H	Boat for sailing the river: same as G but with a mast and a sail.		1
I	Vessels: flat stern; prominent prow; a mast and a sail; a double roofed cabin in the centre; a kiosk on the prow and the stern.	3	

MAP OF THEBES

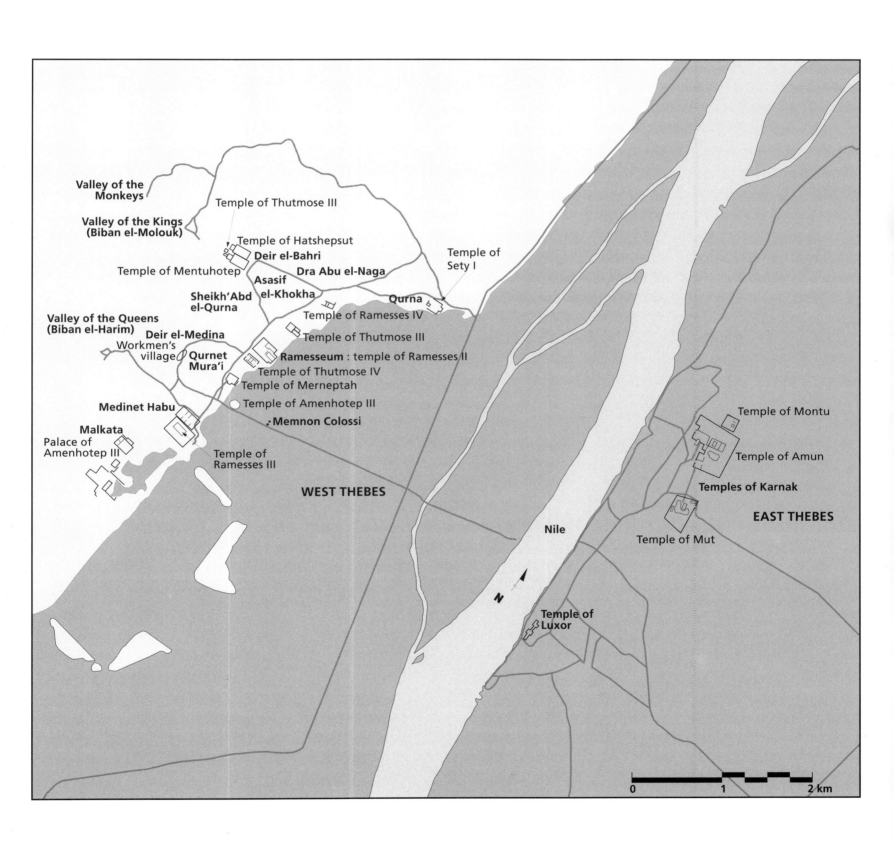

Valley of the
Monkeys

Temple of Thutmose III

Valley of the Kings
(Biban el-Molouk)

Temple of Hatshepsut

Deir el-Bahri

Temple of
Sety I

Temple of Mentuhotep

Dra Abu el-Naga

**Asasif
el-Khokha**

**Sheikh'Abd
el-Qurna**

Qurna

Temple of Ramesses IV

Valley of the Queens
(Biban el-Harim)

Deir el-Medina

Temple of Thutmose III

Workmen's
village

**Qurnet
Mura'i**

Ramesseum : temple of Ramesses II

Temple of Thutmose IV

Temple of Merneptah

Medinet Habu

Temple of Amenhotep III

Malkata

Memnon Colossi

Temple of Montu

Palace of
Amenhotep III

Temple of Amun

Temple of
Ramesses III

Temples of Karnak

WEST THEBES

EAST THEBES

Temple of Mut

Nile

N

Temple of
Luxor

0   1   2 km

LIST OF OBJECTS

Room	N°	Objet	Page
	256b[4]	Flexible vertical strip (gold inlaid with glass and semi-precious stones)	76, 80
	256c to 256-4v	One hundred and four batches of items found on *Tutankhamun's* mummy (various materials)	42, 76, 80, 81
	256k	Dagger (iron blade with handle finishing in a rock crystal pommel and decorated sheath (gold)	80, 118
	256dd	Dagger (gold blade with granulation and inlays) and sheath (gold)	80, *83*, 118
	256fff	**Tit** knot-shaped pendant amulet (gold and carnelian)	76, 81
	256hhh	**Djed** pillar-shaped pendant amulet (gold and faience)	81, 82
	256ppp	Necklace bearing the vulture Nekhbet with closed wings (cloisonné gold set with precious stones)	81, *82*
	256-4o	Royal circlet (gold inlaid with carnelian and glass paste)	76, 80, 81
	257	Figurine placed in the niche against the eastern wall of the **Burial Chamber:** *Osiris*	*73*
	258	Figurine placed in the niche against the western wall of the **Burial Chamber:** *Anubis*	*73*
	259	Figurine placed in the niche against the northern wall of the **Burial Chamber:** a **shabti**	*73*
	260	Figurine placed in the niche against the southern wall of the **Burial Chamber:** a **djed** pillar	*73*
TREASURY	**262**	Scribe's palette bearing Meritaten's name (ivory and six inks)	116, *117*
	266a	Canopy and shrine that protect *Tutankhamun's* Canopic jars (gilt wood inlaid with faience and glass)	*91, 92, 92*
	266b	Canopic shrine divided into four compartments (painted calcite and gilt wood)	*91, 92, 94*
	266c to f	Four lids placed over the compartments holding *Tutankhamun's* internal organs (calcite)	*91, 94, 94*
	266g	Four coffins holding *Tutankhamun's* internal organs (gold inlaid with tainted glass and precious stones)	*91, 94, 98*
	267d	Pectoral decorated with a winged scarab (gold inlaid with precious stones and glass paste)	*98*
	267l	Pectoral decorated with baboons (gold inlaid with precious stones and glass paste)	98, *104*
	269a-1	Pair of earrings: falcon surmounted by a duck head (gold set with glass paste)	98, *104*
	269a-3	Pair of earrings: *Tutankhamun* flanked by two uraei (gold set with glass paste)	98
	269b	Mirror cover in the form of an **ankh** cross (gilt wood)	109
	269d	**Heka** crook, forms a pair with flail no. 269f (gold, copper and glass plate)	*106*, 107
	269e	**Nekhakha** flail, forms a pair with crook no. 269h (gold, copper and glass plate)	107
	269f	**Nekhakha** flail forms a pair with crook no. 269d (gold, copper and glass plate)	*106*, 107
	269h	**Heka** crook forms a pair with flail no. 269e (gold, copper and glass plate)	1067
	271c-d	Mirror case bearing the image of the god *Heh* (gilt wood)	109
	271e[2]	Scribe's palette bearing *Tutankhamun's* name (ivory, two inks and seven calamus)	*117*
	272a	Fan decorated with black and white feathers (ivory)	86
	275a	*Tutankhamun* statue depicted as Ihy, the child god (wood blackened with bitumen or gilt, gold and glass paste)	104, *104*
	289c	*Tutankhamun* statue depicted as Ihy, the child god (wood blackened with bitumen or gilt, gold and glass paste)	104, *104*
	320c	Pendant decorated with the figurine of a kneeling child bearing the royal attributes (gold)	98
	331a	The wooden shabti of *Tutankhamun* presented by **Maya** for his funeral (painted wood)	108, *108*
	333	Undecorated functional chariot for hunting and riding (wood and leather)	49
	335	Quiver (wood decorated with faience, bark and gold elements)	118
	349	Seat decorated with an openwork **sema-tawi** (wood coated with white paint)	52
ANNEXE	**351**	Seat known as the "Episcopal throne" (gold-plated ebony inlaid with fine stones, glass paste, faience and ivory)	52
	379a	Ceremonial shield representing *Tutankhamun* as a sphinx during a war scene (gilt stucco wood)	118
	379b	Ceremonial shield representing *Tutankhamun* hunting a lion (gilt stucco wood)	118
	394	Small receptacle (gold)	113
	403a	Headrest (lapis lazuli blue glass paste)	114
	403b	Headrest (dark blue faience)	114
	403c	Headrest with a support bearing the god Shu (ivory and gold)	114, *114*
	403d	Headrest imitating a folding chair with Bes effigies at the ends (painted ivory)	114
	466	Bed and footboard decorated with the **sema-tawi** and floral motifs (gold-plated ebony)	60
	467	Stool bearing a "golden **sema-tawi**" (gold-plated wood)	52
	469	Pomegranate-shaped vase (incised silver)	113
	578	Ointment vase in the shape of a ceremonial boat (calcite with gilt and painted highlights)	*110*, 112
	579	Ointment vase in the shape of a lion standing (calcite with ivory and painted highlights)	112
	582a	**Khepesh** sword (bronze blade and handle inlaid with wooden elements)	118
	585aa	"Lighter", an item that can produce fire (wood and resin)	113
	586	Folding bed with four pairs of legs (wood)	60
	587	Sleeveless breast-plate (leather)	118
	620:6	Boomerang (elephant tusk and gold)	118
	620:13	Pair of clappers in the shape of an arm (ivory)	116
	620:37	Small receptacle (silver)	113
	620:52	**Khepesh** sword (bronze blade with a handle carved from dark wood)	118

CHRONOLOGY

EARLY DYNASTIC PERIOD
3150-2686 B.C.

1st Dynasty
Narmer
Aha
Djer
Djet
Den
Semerkhet
Qa'a

2nd Dynasty
Hetepsekhemwy
Raneb
Nynetjer
Peribsen
Khasekhemwy

OLD KINGDOM
2686-2181 B.C.

3rd Dynasty
Sanakht
Djoser
Sekhemket
Khaba
Huni

4th Dynasty
Sneferu
Khufu
Djedefra
Khephren
Menkaure
Shepseskaf

5th Dynasty
Userkaf
Sahura
Neferirkara-Kakai
Shepsaskara
Raneferef
Nyuserra
Menkauhor
Djedkara
Unas

6th Dynasty
Teti
Pepy I
Merenra
Pepy II

FIRST INTERMEDIATE PERIOD
2181 - 2060 B.C.

7th Dynasty *(totally unknown)*

8th Dynasty *(from Memphis)*
Wadjkara
Kakara Ibi

9th and 10th Dynasties *(from Herakleopolis)*
Khety I
Merykara
Neferkara
Khety II

11th Dynasty *(Theban and contemporary with the end of the 10th Dynasty)*
Mentuhotep I
Intef I
Intef II
Intef III

MIDDLE KINGDOM
2 060 - 1 782 B.C.

11th Dynasty
Mentuhotep II
Mentuhotep III
Mentuhotep IV

12th Dynasty
Amenemhet I
Senusret I
Amenemhet II
Senwuret II
Senwuret III
Amenemhet III
Amenemhet IV
Sobekneferu

SECOND INTERMEDIATE PERIOD
1782 - 1570 B.C.

13th Dynasty *(a dynasty during which the kings, who are native Egyptians, seem still to reign over the two kingdoms of Egypt, the capital of which is in Iti-Tawi, in the oasis of el-Faiyum)*
Wegaf
Intef IV
Hor
Sebekhotpe II
Khendjer
Sebekhotpe III
Neferhotpe I
Sebekhotpe IV
Aya
Neferhotpe II

14th Dynasty *(contemporary with the end of the 13th Dynasty, which ends in an obscure fashion; the 14th Dynasty only reigns over the eastern part of the Delta)*
Nehesy

15th and 16th Dynasties *(Hyksos dynasties: these kings, coming from the East, take power in Egypt and set up their capital in Avaris)*
Sharek
Yakub-Har
Khyan
Apepi I
Apepi II
Anather
Yakobaam

17th Dynasty *(Theban Dynasty, who tried to win back the land by driving out the Hyksos)*
Sebekemsaf II
Intef VII
Taa I
Taa II
Kamose

NEW KINGDOM
1570 - 1070 B. C.

18th Dynasty

Ahmose
Amenhotep I
Tuthmosis I
Tuthmosis II
Hatshepsut
Tuthmosis III
Amenhotep II
Tuthmosis IV
Amenhotep III
Amenhotep IV-Akhenaten
Smenkhkara
Tutankhamun
Ay
Horemheb

19th Dynasty

Ramesses I
Sethos I
Ramesses II
Merneptah
Amenmessu
Sethos II
Siptah
Tausret

20th Dynasty

Sethnakhte
Ramesses III
Ramesses IV-Ramesses XI

THIRD INTERMEDIATE PERIOD
1070 - 656 B. C.

21st Dynasty *(two contemporary kingdoms: the priests kings usurp the cartouche and reign in Thebes over Upper Egypt, whereas in the Delta, Smendes proclaims himself king at the death of Ramesses XI, sets up his capital in Tanis and reigns over Lower Egypt)*

Tanis	Thebes
Smendes I	Herihor
Amenemnisu	Piankh
Psusennes I	Pinedjem I
Amenemope	Masaharta
Osorkon the Elder	Menkheperre'
Siamun	Smendes II
Psusennes II	Pinedjem II

22nd Dynasty *(Lybian dynasty, coming from Bubastis and reigning in Tanis)*

Sheshonq I
Osorkon I
Sheshonq II
Takelot I
Osorkon II
Takelot II
Sheshonq III
Pimay
Sheshonq V
Osorkon IV
Harsiesis

23rd Dynasty *(contemporary with the end of the 22nd Dynasty, the first ruling in the Delta over Lower Egypt, and the second ruling in Leontopolis over Middle Egypt)*

Pedubastis I
Sheshonq IV
Osorkon III
Takelot III
Rudamon
Iuput

24th Dynasty *(first Dynasty of Sais)*

Tefnakht
Bocchoris

25th Dynasty *(from Nubia: the kings of Napata take over the rule in Egypt)*

Piy
Shabaqo
Shabitqo
Taharqo
Tanutamani

LATE PERIOD
664 - 332 B.C.

26th Dynasty *(second Dynasty of Sais)*

Psamtek I
Nekau
Psamtek II
Apries
Ahmose
Psamtek III

27th Dynasty *(first Persian rule)*

Cambyses
Darius I
Xerxes
Artaxerxes I
Darius II
Artaxerxes II

28th Dynasty Amyrtaios

29th Dynasty Nepherites I
Hakor

30th Dynasty Nectanebo I
Teos
Nectanebo II

31st Dynasty *(second Persian rule)*

Artaxerxes III
Arses
Darius III Codoman

332-323 B.C. *In 332 B.C., Alexander the Great enters into Egypt and frees the country of the Persian rule by chasing Darius III away. At his death in 323, Egypt passes under the government of one of his lieutenants, Ptolemy, who takes the title of pharaoh in 305 and founds the Ptolemaic dynasty.*

305-30 B.C. **Ptolemaic Dynasty**

Ptolemy I Soter I
Ptolemy II Philadelphus
Ptolemy III Euergetes I
Ptolemy IV Philopator
Ptolemy V Epiphanes
Ptolemy VI Philometor
Ptolemy VII Neos Philopator
Ptolemy VIII Euergetes II
Ptolemy IX Soter II
Ptolemy X Alexander I
Ptolemy XI Alexander II
Ptolemy XII Neos Dionysos
Ptolemy XIII and Cleopatra VII
Ptolemy XIV and Cleopatra VII
Cleopatra VII

30 B.C. - 395 A.D. - ROMAN EGYPT

BRIEF LEXICON

AMULETS: these small figurines ensure protection to both the living and the dead. The former wear them on necklaces whilst they are placed in the mummification bandages of the latter. They can be made of faience, precious or semi-precious stones, bronze, gold, silver…, and represent deities, hieroglyphic signs charged with magical powers: the **djed** pillar (durability and stability), the **wadjat**-eye (plenitude), the **ankh** cross (life), the **kheper** scarab (existence) or Isis' **tit** knot (protection under all circumstances).

AMUN: originally from **Thebes**, Amun became the national and dynastic god as from the Middle Kingdom. His main place of worship is **Thebes (Karnak** and **Luxor)** where he is venerated alongside the goddess *Mut* and the god-son *Khonsu.*

ANUBIS: the funerary god is represented by a black jackal or man with a jackal head; he is believed to be the inventor of mummification and, thus, watches over the performance of the embalming rituals. By extension, he becomes the god of the necropolis.

APOPHIS: a giant evil serpent that incarnates the ensemble of destructive forces and the powers of chaos, symbol of evil.

ATEN: he represents the sun disc par excellence. His name appears during the Old Kingdom and is then forgotten until the 18th Dynasty when pharaoh *Akhenaten* names him the dynastic divinity once again.

BA: represented as a bird with a human head, the **ba**, or the soul of the deceased. In certain ways it is a spiritual entity that leaves the body when death takes over and finds its individuality to roam at its leisure. The **ba** can stay in the mausoleum near the body, move in the funerary chapel so as to obtain plentiful offerings, or, even, go out into the fresh air to visit the deceased's favourite places once again.

BASTET: the cat-headed goddess that was venerated in the Delta of **Bubastis**, represents the peaceful aspects of the dangerous goddesses. Her name is symbol of happiness and goodness, thus the important role of her presence in popular culture.

BEARDS: although all respectable Egyptians should be clean-shaven, gods, pharaohs and officials were often represented with a false beard upon their chins symbolising their virile power. The gods' beard was long, thin, finely braided and curved at the end; the kings' was rhomboid and undulating, whilst the nobility simply wore a small goatee beard.

BES: a domestic genius whose image was very popular in households since he was considered to protect women and infants. It was believed that he could chase out the evil spirits and hostile powers with his strange dances.

BOOK OF THE DEAD: more correctly known as **"The book for coming forth by day "**, this compendium of texts (used since the New Kingdom) collects all kinds of formulae that ensure the resurrection of the deceased in the afterlife by giving him or her freedom of movement and granting him or her everything that could be needed in the underworld. The chapters are often decorated with illustrations and are written on a roll of papyrus which is placed in the deceased's sarcophagus or inserted into the mummy's bandages. Many copies of this funerary book have been found, although they are not identical; some present chapters others do not have. To this day, about one hundred and ninety different chapters have been catalogued; numbered from I to CXC.

CANOPIC (JARS): the mummified internal organs of the deceased were stored in four Canopic jars, made of alabaster or calcite, which were under the protection of four gods, known as the *four Sons of Horus,* and four goddesses: *Imsety,* with a human head, and *Isis* watched over the liver; *Hapy,* with a baboon head, and *Nephthys* watched over the lungs; *Duamutef,* with a jackal head, and *Neith* watched over the stomach; *Qebehsenuef,* with a falcon head, and *Selkis* watched over the intestines.

CARTOUCHE: this term refers to the oval-shaped ring that symbolises the universal reign of the king; the fourth and fifth names of the pharaoh are inscribed within: **"He of the sedge and bee"** name and **"Son of Ra"** name.

COSMOGONY: a mythical narrative that recounts the creation of the world and of the different elements of the universe: earth, sky, stars… In Egypt many religious centres have devised their own cosmogony: **Heliopolis, Memphis, Esna, Thebes, Hermopolis**… Each believes in a different creative god, a demiurge, who conceives his or her creation by his or her own means: for example, Ptah creates "by the thought and the verb" and Khnum makes the gods, the beings and all things from his potter's wheel.

COSMOGRAPHY: the scenes that depict the world as the Egyptians believed it to be. They were chased into the walls of the tombs and were called cosmographies. They represented the topography of the Valley of the Nile as the underworld. In the **Valley of the Kings** various tombs offer very complete cosmographies that are collected in the funerary "Books": the **"Book of Gates"** and the **"Book of that which is in the Netherworld."**

CROWN: most of the deities can be identified through the crown they wear. If they did not have this attribute it would often be difficult to distinguish one from another. *Osiris* wears the **atef** crown topped with two feathers; *Horus* the **pschent**, which is a mix of the crowns of Upper and Lower Egypt; *Isis* wears a high backed chair, which symbolises her name; *Maat* and *Shu* wear an ostrich feather; *Selkis* wears a scorpion skin… and so on in the case of each divinity.

DUAT (THE): the Egyptian term used to define the underworld, i.e. the afterlife.

FOUR SONS OF HORUS: these are the "Lords of the Cardinal Points," protectors of the deceased's Canopic jars: *Imsety,* genie of the South; *Duamutef,* genie of the East; *Hapy,* genie of the North and *Qebehsenuef* genie of the West.

GEB: personification of the earth and the wealth the sun contains. *Geb* composes the second divine couple of the Heliopolis Ennead with *Nut,* the sky.

GENIE: the Egyptians defined "genie" as all the beings that, in the underworld, made it difficult and dangerous to access the kingdom of the dead. They are the forces of chaos, hybrid animals, inferior beings and evil forces. They are often depicted armed with pikes and knives that they attack the deceased with. They appear by the hundreds on the walls of the tombs; nonetheless they can be subdued if the deceased knows their name and the words that must be spoken if they are encountered. Hence the reason for their representation being followed by an extremely detailed legend that gives the deceased all information regarding the genie, thus ensuring he will never be caught off guard.

HAPY: personification of the rising of the water level and the flooding of the Nile, guarantee of the fertility of cultivated lands. As a symbol of abundance, *Hapy* is presented as an androgynous divinity, sometimes a male and sometimes a female, with hanging breasts

HARAKHTY: "Horus of the Horizon" is one of the manifestations of the sun god and creator of the **Heliopolis.**

HATHOR: one of the most popular goddesses of the Egyptian pantheon. She has all types of functions, being the goddess of beauty, love, happiness, patron saint of the Theban necropolis, celestial divinity, mistress of foreign countries, royal childminder… With time, her immense popularity allowed her to assimilate the powers of other female divinities, most importantly those of *Isis.*

HEH: god of Eternity, he symbolises "millions of years", i.e. eternal life. He is depicted as a kneeling man holding palm-tree leaves in his hands, a hieroglyphic sign which means "years."

HORUS: son of *Isis* and *Osiris*, became heir to the earthly kingdom through his grandfather *Geb.* Thus, *Horus* is the dynastic god par excellence and the royal function is placed directly under his protection. Also, he is a celestial and sun god, due to which he is associated to the goddess *Hathor,* who became his wife.

IB: hieroglyphic word that means heart.

IHY: the child god of the triad of **Dendera,** believed to be the son of *Hathor* and *Horus.*

ISIS: sister and wife of *Osiris,* mother of *Horus.* Her main feature is her strong personality which gives her different roles: protector of women and children, enchantress par excellence, protector of the deceased mummy, universal goddess…

KA: it is very complicated to render this notion given that there is nothing similar to the Egyptian **ka** in our conception or our language. It is defined as the manifestation of the life-forces, both creative and conservative; it survives the body's physical death. Funerary offerings and formulae are addressed to the **ka** who now becomes an element that allows the deceased to survive in the afterlife.

KHEPRI: the god honoured in **Heliopolis** in the form of a scarab. He symbolises the rising sun that is reborn each morning and along with *Atum,* the setting sun, and *Ra,* the noon sun, he is considered the creative god.

KHNUM: the ram-headed god has many places of veneration. In **Elephantine** he is the patron saint of the cataract and protector of the sources of the Nile alongside *Satis* and *Anukis.* In **Esna,** he is thought of as a creative god: here they believe he created gods, men and all other things from his potter's wheel.

LEGEND OF OSIRIS: this is the most famous myth of Egyptian literature. Unfortunately, only the Greek writer **Plutarch** delivers a full version of the narrative in his book *"From Iside to Osiride".* The Egyptian texts are in very bad condition and present many lacuna. This Heliopolis myth traces the three stages of the life of the gods of the great Ennead: the assassination of *Osiris* by *Seth,* the birth and childhood of *Horus* and the battle between *Horus* and *Seth* for the earthly kingdom.

MAAT: symbol of truth and justice. On the earth she is the guarantor of the cosmic balance and the universal order. In the netherworld she decides the weight of the faults the deceased has committed and the weighing of his/her soul. Both gods and mankind must comply with her rule and respect all that she represents.

MAHE: god represented as a "raging" lion: his function is to battle *Osiris'* enemies. He is worshipped mainly in the Nile Delta.

MASTABA: the term **mastaba,** Arabian for stool, used to designate the civil tombs from the Old Kingdom. These tombs are usually disposed in the necropolis around the royal pyramid and are the resting place of high administrative officials, usually divided into two parts. The superstructure consists of the shrine, for the burial service, and the **serdab,** which holds the deceased's **ka** statue. The infrastructure consists of the well, full of rubble from the funeral, and the vault, which holds the sarcophagus with the deceased's mummy and the burial treasures (furniture, statuettes, ornaments, boats…)

MEHET-WERET: known as the "Great Flood", she appears as a primordial deity swimming in the *Nun* depicted as a cow. She can be associated with other deities of the pantheon: *Isis, Neith, Hathor…*

MUMMIFICATION: the invention and use of the mummification techniques follow an extremely precise logic. In Egypt, death was not the end, but simply a passage towards another form of existence. However, this passage was very dangerous, given that after death the different elements that compose human personality (the **ka,** the **ba,** the name, the body, the heart…) become separated although each conserves its integrity. If the deceased can manage to put them back together, this second life will be possible, thus the body must be conserved as if it decomposes, it will have no chance of survival. Embalming allows for the conservation of the body. The technique used consists of emptying the body of entrails before placing it in natron for sixty-five days to allow it to become dehydrated. Then, it is washed, perfumed and wrapped in bandages between which amulets are inserted. The organs are mummified separately and placed in four Canopic jars set under the protection of the *four Sons of Horus.*

NAOS: this word is used to designate two different things: the first, the stone tabernacle which holds the statue of the god; the second is the room that holds the tabernacle, also called the "Holy of the Holies".

NEFERTUM: the primordial lotus the sun emanated from at the beginning of time. Various divinities are associated to it: in **Memphis,** he is the son of *Ptah* and *Sekhmet,* in **Bubastis** son of the cat-headed goddess *Bastet* and in **Buto** son of the cobra goddess *Wadjit.*

NEITH: she is attributed with various functions; she is the war goddess of the village of **Sais** and the demiurge of the village of **Esna.** In the underworld, she protects the deceased's Canopic jars alongside *Isis, Nephthys* and *Selkis.*

NEKHBET: the vulture goddess from **El-Kab,** her role is to protect Upper Egypt.

NEPHTHYS: she belongs to the last generation of gods from the Heliopolis Ennead, alongside *Osiris, Isis, Horus* the *Ancient* and *Seth.* Her role is essentially funerary and consists in watching over the body of the deceased and his Canopic jars.

NUBIA: this geographical area extends from **Khartoum,** present capital of Sudan, to the Egyptian border. During the pharaonic period, **Nubia** was totally dominated by Egypt and was used as a land of exploitation for their resources of gold, wood, stones, livestock and men; and a transit area towards Africa, in search of ivory, ebony, rare animals and precious essences.

NUN: the original ocean which precedes creation in all cosmogonies and represents the nothingness: *"before the sky existed, before the earth existed, before mankind existed, before death existed"* all that existed was the *Nun.*

NUT: personification of the heavens. In the cosmogony of **Heliopolis** she forms the second divine couple alongside *Geb,* the earth. The diurnal and nocturnal journeys of the sun are made along her body, symbol of the domain along which the sun advances.

OSIRIS: in the Egyptian pantheon, he is the ruler of the Dead as the reborn god, and also plays a primordial role in the yearly regeneration of vegetation. Each person tries to become identified with him in the netherworld and to become part of his kingdom, given that only he can promise an eternal survival.

PTAH: at first his role was patron saint of goldsmiths, sculptors and artisans; he is believed to be the inventor of these techniques. Then, he became the creator of **Memphis** and was associated to the goddess *Sekhmet* and the son god *Nefertum* forming a triad. He then assumed the personality of *Sokaris*, under the name of *Ptah-Sokar-Osiris*, and of *Tatenen*, under the name of *Ptah-Tatenen*.

PYRAMID TEXTS: the funerary texts that are inscribed on the walls of the pyramids of the Old Kingdom. The oldest example dates back to the era of *Unas*, the last pharaoh of the 5th Dynasty. Used by all the sovereigns of the 6th Dynasty, the "Pyramid Texts" disappeared with the upheavals of the First Intermediary Period. They consist of magic formulae, various hymns and religious incantations that should ensure the king's immortality and allow him to identify himself with the sun.

RA: representation of the sun par excellence, he is the most important divinity of the Egyptian pantheon. His main worship place is **Heliopolis**, but he is venerated all over Egypt under different names: *Ra-Harahkty, Amun-Ra, Ra-Atum, Sobek-Ra...*

ROYAL HEAD-CLOTHS: the pharaoh usually wears one of the following head-cloths: a simple wig held by a ribbon; the **afnit**, round-shaped and longer in the back leaving the shoulders uncovered; the **nemes**, a striped cloth which covers the shoulders; the white crown of Upper Egypt; the red crown of Lower Egypt; the **pschent** which is a mixture of the two former crowns; the **khepresh** or war crown which is a type of blue helmet decorated with discs.

ROYAL TITULARITY: consists of five names adopted by the sovereign when he was crowned: the "Horus" name(I), "He of the two ladies" name (II), the "Gold Horus" name (III), "He of the sedge and bee" name (IV), the "Son of Ra" name (V).

SCEPTRES: these complements, carried by gods, pharaohs and nobles determine the qualities and functions of those who hold them. The most commonly-used divine sceptres are the **heka** sceptre (the crook) and the **nekhakha** flagellum (the flail) for *Osiris,* the **wadj** sceptre (papyrus stem-shaped walking stick) for the female deities and the **was** sceptre (the long baton surmounted by a canine-head) for male deities.

SEKHMET: a destructive deity incarnating the sun eye and the dangerous powers. She appears as a lion-headed goddess. In **Memphis** she is associated to the *Ptah* and *Nefertum*, whilst in **Thebes** she is associated to the goddess *Mut* as a warrior goddess.

SELKIS: on earth, this scorpion goddess protects against various bites and stings. In the underworld, she protects the deceased's viscera in the Canopic jars alongside *Isis, Nephthys* and *Neith.*

SEMA-TAWI: the translation of this Egyptian word is *"unification of the Two Lands."* In the iconography, it is symbolised with the two emblematic plants: the lotus of Upper Egypt and the papyrus of Lower Egypt, tied around a trachea by two divinities: *Horus* and *Seth*, or two representations of *Hapy*. The hieroglyphic symbol of the trachea means "to join." Thus the **sema-tawi** represents that unification of the South and the North under one kingdom.

SETH: this mythical animal-headed god is charged with different functions, some positive and some negative. He is both protector of the sun boat and the murderer of *Osiris*. In Lower Egypt he symbolises "the Foreigner" and "the Invader": he incarnates the forces of evil, chaos and trouble.

SHABTI: this mummiform statue is placed in the tomb and is charged with carrying out the deceased's tasks and chores in the netherworld. His body is inscribed with a few words: *"Oh shabti! If X (the deceased) is required to carry out chores in the underworld... you will say: Present!"* These statues appeared in the Middle Kingdom, and depending on the position of the deceased they can be made of wood, bronze, faience, stone or clay. Sometimes they can be found in tombs by the hundreds.

SHU: he forms the first divine couple of the **Heliopolis** cosmogony with *Tefnut*. They are both born from the sun god and with their powers they allow him to reveal himself. *Shu*, in particular, is god of space and air and symbol of the breath of life.

SPHINX: this lion with a human head called sphinx generally symbolises the king or a sun deity. As the incarnation of the pharaoh his function is battling the enemies and guarding the benevolent. When he represents a sun god on earth, he watches over the western regions which the sun and the deceased pass through. The **Giza** sphinx belongs to the second category of sphinxes: he represents *Harmakhis*, "*Horus* in the Horizon," and *Hurun*, a Canaanitic god assimilated to Harmakhis as from the New Kingdom.

TAWERET: she has no special worship place but she is venerated in all Egyptian households as the goddess who protects pregnant women and children.

THOTH: he sometimes appears as an ibis and others as a baboon. He has multiple functions and his powers are diverse: he is the moon god, the inventor of writing and of the sciences, the protector of scribes, master of knowledge, messenger and the divine clerk... In the netherworld, he watches over the correct weighing of the deceased's soul and inscribes the verdict on the sacred tablets.

TRIAD: a group of deities from the same village who compose a family scheme: god, goddess and son-god or daughter-goddess. The most famous triads are *Ptah, Sekhmet* and *Nefertum* in **Memphis**, *Amun, Mut* and *Khonsu* in **Thebes**, *Hathor, Horus* and *Ihy* in **Dendera**, *Khnum, Satis* and *Anukis* in **Elephantine** and *Osiris, Isis* and *Horus* in **Abydos**.

URAEUS: this term designates the cobra, the eye of Ra from the Heliopolis legend, which surmounts the royal head-cloth. It is believes to protect the god in all places and circumstances, *"even during the night when he is sleeping,"* and fights off all his enemies.

WADJIT: the cobra goddess form **Buto**, her role is to protect Lower Egypt.

WEIGHING OF THE SOUL: this refers to chapter CXXV of the "Book of the Dead." Passage in which the deceased, introduced by *Anubis* faces the tribunal of gods whilst his or her heart is placed on one of the plates of the scales, and *Maat*, symbol of justice, is on the other. *Thoth* watches over this operation, and it is he who must determine if the deceased is worthy of entering the kingdom of *Osiris*. A monstrous being (the "Devourer of the dead") is at the foot of the scales, ready to jump on the deceased if the judgement is unfavourable.

WRITING: Egyptians traditionally used three forms of writing: the **hieroglyphic**, a sacred writing, remarkable in its designs and exquisiteness; and two simple forms of writing: the **hieratic**, and the **demotic**, which replaced it in the Seventeenth Century B.C.

129

BIBLIOGRAPHY

Cyril Aldred,
The Egyptians, Thames and Hudson, London / New York, 1961 / 1984

John Baines et Jaromir Malek,
Atlas of Ancient Egypt, Andromeda, Oxford, 1980 and 1996

Lord Carnarvon and Howard Carter,
Five Years Explorations at Thebes, a record of work done, 1907-1911,
Oxford, 1911

Howard Carter,
The tomb of Tutankhamen,
Phyllis J. Walker, 1954

Howard Carter and Arthur Mace,
The tomb of Tut-ankh-amen,
Cassel & Co., London, 1923-1933

Peter A. Clayton,
Chronicle of the Pharaohs,
Thames and Hudson, London, 1994 and 1999

Marc Collier and Bill Manley,
How to read Egyptian hieroglyphs,
British Museum Press, London, 1998 and 1999

Christiane Desroches-Noblecourt,
Toutankhamon, vie et mort d'un pharaon,
Pygmalion, 1988

Raymond O. Faulkner,
The Ancient Egyptian Book of the Dead,
under the management of C. Andrews, London, 1985 and 1996

Raymond O. Faulkner,
The Ancient Egyptian Pyramid Texts (two volumes), Oxford, 1969

Penelope Fox,
Tutankhamun's treasure,
Oxford University Press, London, 1951

Henri Frankfort,
Ancient Egyptian Religion, New York, 1948

Sir Allan Gardiner,
Egypt of the Pharaohs, Oxford / New York, 1961

John Gwyn Griffiths,
The conflict of Horus and Seth from Egyptian and Classical sources,
Liverpool, 1960

John Gwyn Griffiths,
Plutarch's De Iside et Osiride, Swansea, 1970

George Hart,
Egyptian myths, British museum Press

Herodotus,
Histories, Book II, A. B. Lloyd,
Herodotus Book II.1: an intoduction (Leiden, 1975)
Herodotus Book II.2: commentary 1-98 (Leiden, 1976)
Herodotus Book II.2: commentary 99-182 (Leiden, 1988)

Erik Hornung,
Der Eine und die Vielen, Darmstadt, 1971

Claire Lalouette,
Textes sacrés et textes profanes de l'Ancienne Égypte,
Connaissances de l'Orient, Gallimard UNESCO, Paris, 1984

Mark Lehner,
The complete Pyramids, Thames and Hudson, London

Siegfried Morenz,
Osiris und Amun, Kult und Heilige Stätten, Munich, 1966

Georges Posener, Serge Sauneron et Jean Yoyotte,
Dictionnaire de la civilisation égyptienne, Hazan, 1959

Donald B. Redford,
Akhénaton, the heretic king, Princeton, 1995

Nicholas Reeves,
The complete Tutankhamun,
Thames and Hudson, London, 1990

Nicholas Reeves and Richard H. Wilkinson,
The complete Valley of the Kings,
Thames and Hudson, London

Serge Sauneron et Jean Yoyotte,
La naissance du monde selon l'Égypte ancienne,
Sources Orientales I, Seuil, Paris, 1959

Ian Shaw et Paul Nicholson,
British Museum, Dictionary of Ancient Egypt,
British Museum Press, 1995

Jacques Vandier,
Manuel d'archéologie égyptienne,
Éditions A. et J. Picard & Cie, Paris, 1952 à 1964